I Can't Believe
It's
Keto!

60 Incredible
**Low-Carb Recipes for Pizzas,
Breads, Lasagnas and More**

I Can't Believe

It's Keto!

Leili Malakooti
Creator of Leili_Keto

PAGE STREET
PUBLISHING CO.

PAGE STREET
PUBLISHING CO.

First published in 2021 by

Page Street Publishing Co.

27 Congress Street, Suite 105

Salem, MA 01970

www.pagestreetpublishing.com

Distributed by Macmillan, sales in Canada by The Canadian Manda Group.

25   24   23   22 21   1   2   3   4   5

ISBN-13: 978-1-64567-342-2

ISBN-10: 1-64567-342-1

Library of Congress Control Number: 2020948811

Cover and book design by Page Street Publishing Co. and Leili Malakooti

Photography by Leili Malakooti

Printed and bound in the United States

To Kaveh, my dear husband.

My vision of a beautiful keto cookbook would still
be a dream without your constant support! Thank you for
encouraging me to become what my heart sees!

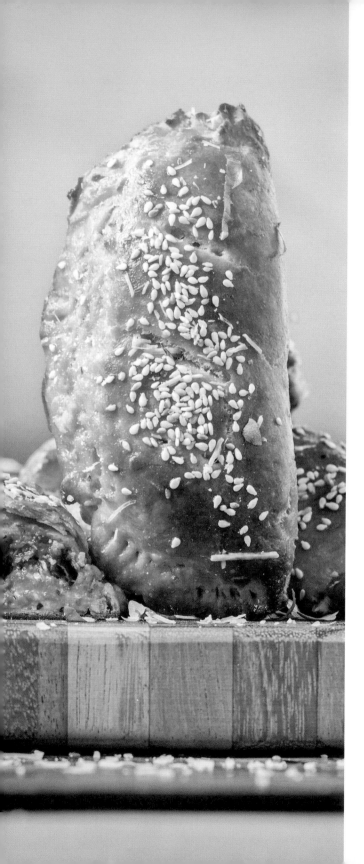

Contents

Introduction

Are you missing variety in your keto foods? Are you looking for that family-favorite dish or a special holiday treat? Are you missing the great pastries and breads that you love? Are you tired of cooking separately for family or guests so that you can stick to your diet? Sure, the keto diet makes you feel energetic, healthier and calmer—but do you think you have to give up all that you love? I did, and I found my successful keto diet *boring* at first. But guess what?

Keto does not have to be boring!

Here's what you'll find in this cookbook:

Food you can (and want to!) eat on your keto diet.
Food you can serve for a party.
Food that is beautiful.
Food that your family and friends can enjoy.
Well-tested recipes that really work.

And you won't even believe that they are keto!

After losing 100 pounds (45 kg) on a very basic keto plan, I knew I had to find a more interesting way to stay in ketosis to keep my prediabetic tendencies in check. One serious health scare was enough! For a person who grew up in a family of great cooks and bakers, this was a challenge. I've always loved to cook, and I loved celebrating life with good food at my mother's Persian table. Why shouldn't I cook and eat delicious, beautiful food that delights the senses?

My kitchen became my laboratory, where I tested and experimented with keto-friendly ingredients and products. I had to find not just an acceptable recipe but the *best* recipe and technique; I wanted excellence, not nutty or "fathead" versions of the dishes I love.

Finally, I am ready to call these recipes, breads and doughs a success!

It has been my joy to create fusion dishes for you from my Iranian heritage but also from the other places I have lived and worked as a graphic designer for the past 15 years—the Middle East, Pacific regions and now the United States. The unique flavors and combinations you find in these chapters are fully adapted for your keto needs. Because I want you to be successful when you try these recipes, I have included tips and photographs to guide you.

I have remained in ketosis for more than 5 years while experimenting with creating delicious recipes. I have photographed my dishes and shared my creations with an international keto community via my Instagram account (@leili_keto) and have many enthusiastic keto followers who enjoy my recipes. Now it's time to share what I've learned with *you* to help you be successful in your keto journey and to live joyfully in a healthy way.

I believe that we eat with all our senses.
We eat with our eyes,
Our noses,
Our palates,
Our teeth and tongues.
When these senses are satisfied, we don't miss the heavy carbohydrates that once filled our plates.

Leili Malakooti

Sensational Feasts

and Weeknight Favorites

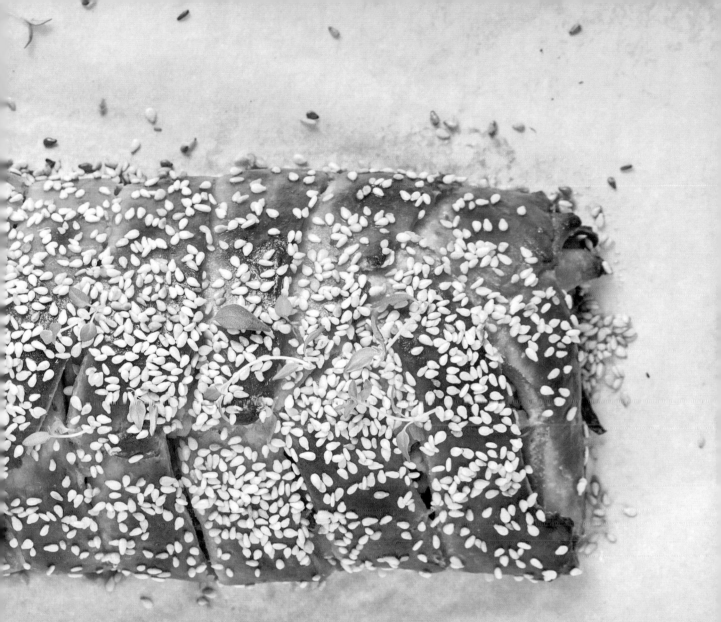

Family favorites like pizza, calzones and chicken paprikash fit perfectly with the keto lifestyle thanks to the variations and adaptations I have developed over time. This chapter provides you with beloved classics you can enjoy on any weeknight, as well as international dishes for special occasions. Some are foods you've seen before and others will be welcome new additions.

I love to invite people to share my table, my heritage and my cooking skills—but I don't want them to worry about my keto diet. You will be so pleased to use these recipes for family dinners or celebrations, and no one will suspect that they are keto! Enjoy!

Keto **Beef Wellington**

Special occasions call for special meals—and are also perilous times for your low-carb diet. Thankfully, this keto take on a classic British centerpiece entrée has you covered. Inspired by Gordon Ramsay's Beef Wellington recipe, this starts with a good-quality beef tenderloin, which is seared and wrapped in a flavorful mushroom paste called a duxelles, then in prosciutto and finally in a pastry jacket. The result is a visual and savory delight—a keto masterpiece!

Serves 10   Total carbs: 7 g   Net carbs: 2 g   Fat: 36 g   Protein: 72 g

1 center-cut beef tenderloin, about 1 ½ lb (680 g)

Kosher salt and freshly ground black pepper

2 tbsp (30 ml) avocado oil

2 tbsp (32 g) Dijon mustard

4 tbsp (56 g) unsalted butter

1 lb (454 g) fresh mushrooms (cremini or shiitake), cleaned, trimmed and chopped into small pieces

1 medium shallot

3 cloves garlic, minced

1 tsp finely minced fresh thyme leaves

¼ cup (60 ml) cognac or other brandy or barrel-aged spirit such as bourbon

¼ cup (60 ml) heavy cream

¼ tsp salt

½ tsp black pepper

To ensure even cooking, tie the beef tenderloin every 2 inches (5 cm) with butcher's twine. Season the meat liberally with salt and pepper.

Heat a tablespoon or two (15 or 30 ml) of avocado oil in a large pan over high heat. Sear the filet in the pan on all sides until well browned, 2 minutes per side, about 12 minutes total. Do not move the filet until it is brown.

Remove the filet from the pan and let it cool. When the beef is cool enough to handle, after about 15 minutes, trim the strings from the beef and brush the filet on all sides with the Dijon mustard. Place it in the refrigerator to cool further.

Meanwhile, in a pan, melt the butter over medium heat, then add the mushrooms and stir. Allow the mushrooms to exude their excess water and cook it off. The mushrooms should start to brown and maybe stick to the pan a little bit. This will take about 12 minutes.

When the mushrooms are browning, add the shallot, garlic and thyme and stir. Cook until the shallot softens and becomes translucent, about 5 minutes. Add the cognac to the mushrooms and cook for a few minutes, stirring some, until the cognac is almost completely cooked off.

Add the heavy cream and cook, stirring occasionally, until the cream thickens, about 5 minutes. Add the salt and pepper.

Transfer the duxelles (mushroom mixture) to a dish and refrigerate it for 30 minutes.

(continued)

8 paper-thin slices prosciutto

Oat fiber flour, for dusting

1 sheet Leili's Perfect Pastry Dough (page 68), plus 1 sheet for lattice decoration (optional)

2 egg yolks, beaten, for egg wash, divided

Coarse salt

1 bunch (57 g) fresh thyme sprigs, for garnish

Roll out a large piece of plastic wrap. Lay out the slices of prosciutto on the plastic wrap so the long pieces overlap. Spread the mushroom mixture over the prosciutto. Place the beef filet in the middle, then roll the mushroom and prosciutto over the filet, using the plastic wrap so that you do this tightly.

Wrap up the beef filet into a tight barrel shape, twisting the ends of the plastic wrap to secure it. Chill it in the freezer for 1 hour.

Preheat the oven to 375°F (190°C). On a lightly floured surface, roll out the sheet of Leili's Perfect Pastry Dough to a size that will wrap around the beef filet.

Unwrap the filet from the plastic wrap and place it in the middle of the pastry dough. Brush the edges of the pastry with the beaten egg yolks. Fold the pastry around the filet, cutting off any excess at the ends (pastry that is more than two layers thick will not cook all the way, so try to limit the overlap).

Place the wrapped filet on a small plate, seam side down, and brush the beaten egg yolks all over the top. Or if you are adding a decorative lattice top, wait to add the egg wash to the base pastry until just before you put on the lattice top. Chill it for 15 to 20 minutes. Place the pastry-wrapped filet on a baking pan. Brush the exposed surface again with the beaten eggs.

Score the top of the pastry with a sharp knife, not going all the way through the pastry. Sprinkle the top with coarse salt. If decorating with lattice, roll out another piece of Leili's Perfect Pastry Dough on a lightly floured surface. Carefully roll a lattice cutter lengthwise over the dough to cut through it thoroughly. Pull the lattice gently to separate the diamond shapes, using a knife tip to loosen if necessary.

When your lattice is ready, brush the egg wash on the base pastry then gently lift the lattice onto the surface of the Beef Wellington. Tuck the pastry down around the ends to secure. After it is placed where you would like it, brush the lattice with the egg wash as well.

Bake it for 35 to 45 minutes. After 15 minutes cover the top loosely with a sheet of foil. The pastry should be nicely golden when it is done. To ensure that your roast is medium rare, test it with an instant-read meat thermometer. Remove the Keto Beef Wellington from the oven at 125 to 130°F (52 to 54°C) for medium rare. Allow the Beef Wellington to rest for 10 minutes before cutting off the ends and slicing it to serve. Garnish it with the fresh thyme sprigs.

Mangia! Lasagna with Protein Noodles

Lasagna is the perfect dish for serving a crowd—but all the carbs that make it so good are obviously not keto friendly. The secret to a good keto lasagna is the low-carb, protein-filled lasagna noodles that are the perfect base for melty cheese and spicy sauce. This is a dish everyone will enjoy, keto or not. *Mangia!* Eat!

Serves 9   Total carbs: 8 g   Net carbs: 6 g   Fat: 26 g   Protein: 27 g

Protein Noodles

1 cup (100 g) almond flour

2 tbsp (18 g) golden flaxseed

1 scoop (30 g) whey isolate, plus extra for rolling the dough

½ tsp salt

1 tsp xanthan gum

1 large egg

2 tbsp (30 ml) warm water (100–110°F [38–43°C])

Meat Sauce

¼ cup (13 g) onion, minced

2 tbsp (30 ml) avocado oil

1 lb (454 g) ground beef

¼ cup (25 g) chopped green bell pepper (optional)

1 cup (225 g) sugar-free marinara sauce

1 tsp Italian seasoning

Salt and pepper

To prepare the protein noodles, whisk together the almond flour, golden flaxseed, whey isolate, salt and xanthan gum in a large mixing bowl. Add the egg and water. Use a spatula to mix it all together and use your hands to continue kneading it into a ball. Roll the noodle dough between two sheets of parchment paper using a rolling pin. Dust the dough with whey isolate if it is too sticky.

Make sure the dough is rolled to about ¼ inch (6 mm) thick or slightly thinner. Use a knife or pizza cutter to cut out several rectangles the length of your casserole dish.

To prepare the meat sauce, add the onion, avocado oil, ground beef and bell pepper (if using) to a large skillet. Cook over medium heat until the meat is browned, about 10 minutes.

Add the marinara sauce, Italian seasoning, salt and pepper. Reduce to low heat and cook at a simmer for about 5 minutes.

(continued)

Ricotta Mixture

1 cup (246 g) ricotta cheese

¼ cup (25 g) grated Parmesan cheese, plus more for serving

1 egg

¼ tsp salt

¼ tsp garlic powder

¼ cup (8 g) chopped baby spinach (optional)

1 cup (83 g) shredded mozzarella cheese, for assembling

Italian seasoning (optional)

Fresh basil, oregano and parsley, finely chopped, for serving (optional)

In a bowl, mix the ricotta cheese, Parmesan and egg with the salt and garlic powder, then add the chopped spinach, if using.

Preheat the oven to 350°F (177°C).

Evenly slice the protein noodle dough into thirds. The slices should just fit into a 5 x 9–inch (13 x 23–cm) loaf pan or a 9 x 9–inch (23 x 23–cm) casserole pan.

Spoon a thin layer of meat sauce onto the bottom of the pan. Add a noodle layer over the meat sauce.

Add one-third of the remaining meat sauce across the noodle layer. Spread 3 tablespoons (45 g) of the ricotta cheese mixture across the filling and sprinkle some mozzarella cheese on top.

Repeat with the second noodle, meat sauce, ricotta and mozzarella layers, using up the rest of the ricotta.

Add the third noodle layer. Top with the remaining meat sauce. Sprinkle on the remaining mozzarella. If desired, you can add a pinch of Italian seasoning to the cheese.

Bake the lasagna in the middle of your oven for about 25 minutes, then broil it for 2 minutes to allow the cheese to brown.

Let the lasagna cool slightly before slicing and serving. If desired, sprinkle on some finely chopped fresh basil, oregano and parsley and freshly grated Parmesan cheese before serving.

Leili's Crispy Fried Chicken

Tempted by those intriguing fried chicken aromas as you drive by your favorite fast food places? Here's the perfect family-pleasing recipe to satisfy both your keto diet and your taste for fast food. The secret is a well-seasoned buttermilk used to marinate the meat; repeating the seasonings in a whey protein coating keeps the chicken pieces moist and tasty while frying.

Serves **6**   Total carbs: **5 g**   Net carbs: **5 g**   Fat: **21 g**   Protein: **56 g**

1 tsp salt

1 tsp dried thyme leaves

1 tsp dried sage leaves

1 tsp dried oregano leaves

½ tbsp (8 g) celery salt

1 tbsp (7 g) ground black pepper

½ tbsp (3 g) dried mustard

1 tbsp (7 g) paprika

½ tsp garlic powder

1 tsp ground ginger

1 tbsp (7 g) ground white pepper

¼ cup (25 g) arrowroot flour

1½ cups (150 g) unflavored whey protein powder

2 cups (470 ml) full fat buttermilk

1 large egg

2 lb (908 g) chicken drumsticks, breast, tenders or thighs

Avocado oil or ghee, for frying

Using a food processor or blender, mix the salt, thyme, sage, oregano, celery salt, black pepper, dried mustard, paprika, garlic powder, ginger and white pepper, blending until they are well mixed and the herbs are well crushed. Divide the mixture evenly into two large bowls. Add the arrowroot flour and the whey protein powder to the first bowl containing one-half of the herbs and spices and mix with a whisk. Set this aside to use as a coating for the chicken after it marinates.

Add the buttermilk and egg to the second bowl with the other half of the herbs and spices and whisk until combined. Add the chicken to the buttermilk mixture and refrigerate the marinating chicken for at least 4 hours or overnight.

Remove the chicken from the mixture and let any excess buttermilk drip off. Dredge the chicken pieces in the flour mixture on all sides, then shake off the excess coating. Let it rest on a baking sheet for 20 to 30 minutes.

Add the oil to a deep fryer or a large pot that is at least 5 inches (13 cm) high so that the chicken can be fully submerged. Heat the oil to 325°F (165°C) and fry the chicken in small batches. Fry the largest pieces for up to 18 minutes, the wings for 8 to 10 minutes and the drumsticks for 12 to 15 minutes depending on size. I use a meat thermometer to test the pieces and remove them when they reach an internal temperature of 165°F (74°C). Remove the chicken from the oil and add it to a drying rack on top of a clean baking sheet.

Serve two or three pieces per person. Store any leftover chicken in the fridge in an airtight container and then reheat it gently in the microwave for 30 to 45 seconds to eat later. The chicken should still be nice and crunchy even as leftovers.

Hearty Chicken Calzones

Who doesn't love a packable meal with lots of flavor? These chicken calzones can be made ahead for a work lunch, party food or a "ready when you are" food for the grab-and-go eater. Homemade calzones pack chicken, vegetables and pizza sauce into a keto-friendly crust—irresistible! You'll love how my Perfect Pastry Dough (page 68) tastes in this family dish!

Serves 6   Total carbs: 12 g   Net carbs: 6 g   Fat: 34 g   Protein: 34 g

---

1 cup (250 g) fresh ricotta

4 oz (112 g) fresh mozzarella, grated

½ cup (46 g) grated Parmesan cheese, divided

3 tbsp (4 g) chopped basil

1 tsp Italian seasoning, plus more for seasoning

Salt and pepper, to taste

2 tbsp (28 g) salted butter

3 cloves garlic, minced

1 tsp minced fresh rosemary leaves

1 cup (70 g) sliced mushrooms

2 cups (280 g) cooked chicken, shredded

¼ cup (25 g) chopped green bell pepper

½ cup (112 g) sugar-free marinara sauce

1 sheet Leili's Perfect Pastry Dough (page 68)

1 egg, beaten, for egg wash, divided

In a medium bowl, combine the ricotta, mozzarella, ¼ cup (23 g) of the Parmesan cheese, basil and Italian seasoning. Lightly season the cheese mixture with salt and pepper.

In a large skillet over medium heat, melt the butter. Add the garlic and rosemary and stir it briefly until it is fragrant, about 30 seconds. Add the mushrooms and stir to coat them evenly in butter. Season with salt and pepper and continue cooking, stirring occasionally, until the mushrooms are lightly golden, 6 to 8 minutes. Add the cooked shredded chicken and green bell pepper and stir in the marinara sauce. At this point, set the chicken mixture aside to cool completely.

Preheat the oven to 365°F (185°C) and line a baking tray with a baking mat or parchment paper.

Take the sheet of Leili's Perfect Pastry Dough, divide it into six equal portions, then roll each portion into a circle about 5 inches (13 cm) wide. You can play with the thickness here, but I like to roll it out nice and thin. If the dough feels very soft and warm at this point, chill it in the refrigerator for another 30 minutes before baking.

Spread the ricotta cheese mixture onto one-half of the circle, leaving a ½-inch (1.3-cm) border around the edges. Follow with the chicken mixture and any other toppings you desire. I prefer to add more Parmesan cheese. Fold the non-filled side of the dough over the filling to form a half-circle shape. Brush the edges with the egg wash to help them stick together during baking. Seal the edges of the calzone by folding the dough over and pinching it. Make a small slit in the calzone using a sharp knife to let steam escape.

Brush the top with more egg wash. Sprinkle each calzone with 2 teaspoons (4 g) of Parmesan and additional herbs (if desired), then bake each calzone until it is golden brown and cooked through, 18 to 20 minutes. The cooled calzones can be wrapped for storage in the refrigerator for up to 3 days. Reheat them in a 350°F (177°C) oven for 5 to 8 minutes.

Date Night Chicken Mushroom Strudel

Sometimes you just need a quiet dinner for two with a special dish that can be enjoyed by the eyes and the palate. Rich flavors in the chicken filling complement the keto-perfect pastry dough, and the golden braided crust is a feast to behold. What a way to make a special night!

Serves 8   Total carbs: 10 g   Net carbs: 5 g   Fat: 56 g   Protein: 25 g

---

2 tbsp (30 ml) extra virgin olive oil, for frying

4 cloves garlic, peeled and chopped

8 oz (226 g) mushrooms, sliced

⅓ cup (80 ml) white wine

4 oz (112 g) cream cheese

3 tbsp (45 ml) sour cream

2 sage leaves

2 sprigs thyme, plus extra to decorate

Salt and pepper, to taste

2 cups (280 g) cooked chicken, shredded

1 sheet Leili's Perfect Pastry Dough (page 68)

¼ cup (23 g) grated Parmesan cheese

1 egg yolk, beaten with 1 tsp water, for egg wash

1 tbsp (9 g) sesame seeds

Heat the olive oil in a large pan over medium heat, then add the garlic and cook it for about 1 minute. Add the mushrooms and continue frying for another 5 minutes. Add the white wine, cream cheese, sour cream, sage leaves and thyme and cook, stirring, until it becomes a creamy mixture and the mushrooms are cooked through, about 5 minutes. Season with salt and pepper to taste. Add the shredded chicken and cool it completely. You can also do this step the day ahead.

Preheat the oven to 350°F (177°C). Line a baking tray with a baking mat or parchment paper.

Roll out the pastry dough into a 12 x 8–inch (30 x 20–cm) rectangle on a lightly floured surface. Transfer the sheet of dough to the baking tray.

Spoon the chicken and mushroom mixture onto the center of the pastry rectangle and sprinkle it with the Parmesan cheese. With the long side of the pastry facing you, cut six to eight slits into both short ends of the pastry to make approximately 1-inch (2.5-cm)-wide strips that can make a covering for the filling. Bring the strips over the filling, "braiding" the alternating strips. Brush the top with the beaten egg and water and sprinkle the sesame seeds over the egg wash.

Bake the strudel until it is golden brown and crispy, about 25 to 30 minutes. Let the chicken pastry cool slightly before slicing and serving it.

Elegant Salmon in Pastry

There's something about pastry-wrapped food that gives it a little mystery and makes it something to anticipate. Cooks also know that the pastry helps fish stay moist in the oven, and the delicate flavors of wine, za'atar and cheeses give this special salmon dish an extra elegant taste. My husband tells me he could eat salmon three times a week, and this is one of his favorites. Try this in the spring when asparagus is in season!

Serves 6   Total carbs: 10 g   Net carbs: 6 g   Fat: 89 g   Protein: 40 g

1 lb (454 g) salmon fillet

Salt and pepper

¼ lb (112 g) fresh asparagus, trimmed

2 tbsp (28 g) salted butter

1 shallot, chopped

2 cloves garlic, minced

2 tbsp (30 ml) white wine

5 oz (140 g) cream cheese

5 oz (140 g) fresh baby spinach, chopped

¼ cup (25 g) grated Parmesan cheese

1 sheet Leili's Perfect Pastry Dough (page 68)

Oat fiber flour, for dusting

1 tsp za'atar

1 egg, beaten, for egg wash

Preheat the oven to 375°F (190°C) and line a baking sheet with parchment paper.

Season the salmon with salt and pepper. Cut the tips off the asparagus. Reserve the stems. Heat the butter, shallot and garlic in a large pan over medium heat. Sauté until the shallot becomes translucent.

Bring the heat to high and add the white wine. Let the liquid cook off for about 5 minutes, then add the cream cheese and sauté for 1 minute. Last, add the spinach and Parmesan cheese. Sauté just until the spinach softens. Let this mixture cool completely.

Roll out the pastry dough into a 12 x 8–inch (30 x 20–cm) rectangle on a lightly floured piece of parchment paper or lightly floured silicone baking mat. Divide the sheet into two sections, each 6 x 8 inches (15 x 20 cm). Transfer one sheet of dough to the baking sheet. Lay the salmon on the pastry in the pan, sprinkle the za'atar on top of the salmon, then spread it with the spinach and cream cheese mixture. Lay the raw stems of asparagus on top, like pencils.

Brush the margins of the pastry with the egg wash. Lay the second sheet of pastry over the salmon and press the edges to seal, like a giant ravioli. Trim the edges, leaving a 1-inch (2.5-cm) border. Press the border with the tines of a fork, then, with the dull edge of a knife, scallop the edges. Make two or three slits in the top of the pastry to allow the steam to escape. Brush the pastry all over with the egg wash and bake it until it is puffed up and golden brown, about 20 minutes.

Remove the pastry from the oven and let it cool for 5 minutes before slicing. This dish is also good at room temperature.

Royal Shrimp Rice (*Meigoo Polo*)

Every Persian family knows this traditional dish with aromatic rice and spicy shrimp. Cayenne pepper gives this dish its spicy kick, but it can be adjusted (or even omitted) to your family's taste. An easy substitution of cauliflower rice complements the aromatic shrimp for a low-carb, tasty balance of flavors and textures. This luxurious keto dish is fit for a king!

Serves 6   Total carbs: 7.7 g   Net carbs: 5 g   Fat: 6.2 g   Protein: 8.5 g

---

3 tbsp (42 g) butter, divided (can substitute avocado oil)

6 cups (600 g) riced cauliflower

1 tbsp (15 ml) white vinegar

½ tsp salt, plus more to taste

Pepper, to taste

1 yellow onion, finely chopped

4 cloves garlic, chopped

1 tsp tomato paste

1 tsp turmeric

¼ tsp cayenne pepper, or to taste

1 tsp ground cumin

1 lb (454 g) shrimp, peeled and deveined

½ cup (30 g) fresh cilantro, chopped

¼ tsp saffron, ground and dissolved in 1 tbsp (15 ml) hot water (optional)

Heat 1 tablespoon (14 g) of the butter or avocado oil in a large pan over medium heat. Add the riced cauliflower and white vinegar and sauté for 5 to 7 minutes. Season to taste with salt and pepper and set it aside.

Heat the remaining 2 tablespoons (28 g) of butter or avocado oil in another pan. Add the onion and sauté over medium heat until it is golden brown, about 5 minutes.

Stir in the garlic and cook for 1 minute.

Add in the tomato paste, turmeric, the ½ teaspoon salt and cayenne pepper. Stir well to mix the ingredients.

Stir in the cumin and add the shrimp. Cook for about 2 minutes, stirring to coat the shrimp with the spices. Continue to cook over medium heat until the shrimp is pink and fully cooked, 10 to 12 minutes, then add the chopped cilantro.

Meigoo Polo is traditionally served from a large platter. As a last step, sprinkle the saffron mixture over the shrimp and rice in the serving dish and mix it lightly with two large forks. Enjoy the signature aromas!

Serve immediately.

Pizza *Bianca*

We love family-friendly pizza, but sometimes you just need pizza for adults. My keto Versatile Naan (page 59) makes a perfect crust for a sophisticated pizza and is strong enough to hold the hearty filling of this version. The combination of cheeses and bacon is a refreshing change from tomato-based pizza. Add a little salad on top, dressed to perfection with garlic and oil, for the ideal keto meal!

Serves 8   Total carbs: 11 g   Net carbs: 6 g   Fat: 20 g   Protein: 29 g

---

2 tsp (10 ml) extra virgin olive oil, plus more for brushing

4 cloves garlic, crushed

1/3 cup (83 g) full fat ricotta cheese

1 cup (162 g) cottage cheese

2 tsp (2 g) chopped fresh thyme

1/4 tsp freshly ground black pepper

1/4 cup (23 g) grated Parmesan cheese

2 slices cooked bacon, chopped

1 batch Versatile Naan dough (page 59)

Coconut flour, for flouring the dough

3 oz (84 g) fresh mozzarella cheese, very thinly sliced

3 oz (84 g) prosciutto (about 7 slices)

1 tsp fresh lemon juice

1 tsp balsamic vinegar

1 1/2 cups (30 g) baby arugula

Preheat the oven to 450°F (232°C). When the oven is preheated, add a pizza stone to heat. Leave the stone in the oven until it is very hot and the dough is ready to bake.

Heat a small skillet over medium heat. Add the olive oil to the pan and swirl to coat. Add the garlic and cook it for 2 minutes or until the garlic is lightly browned. Remove the garlic with a slotted spoon. Finely chop the garlic. Reserve the oil.

Place the cooked garlic, ricotta cheese, cottage cheese, thyme, pepper and Parmesan cheese in a medium bowl. Beat with a mixer at medium-high speed until almost smooth, about 2 minutes. Add the cooked bacon and mix.

Roll the dough into a 14-inch (35-cm) circle or rectangle shape on a lightly floured surface. Pierce the entire surface of the dough liberally with a fork. Carefully remove the hot pizza stone from the oven.

Carefully arrange the dough on the pizza stone. Brush the dough lightly with olive oil, making sure to coat the edges. Bake the pizza for 5 minutes to partially cook the crust.

Spread the cottage cheese mixture over the crust, leaving a 1/2-inch (1.3-cm) border. Arrange the mozzarella over the cottage cheese mixture and place the prosciutto on top. Lower the heat of the oven slightly to 430°F (220°C) and bake the pizza for 8 minutes or until the crust and cheese are browned.

Combine the reserved garlic oil, lemon juice and balsamic vinegar in a medium bowl. Add the arugula and toss to coat. Top the pizza with the arugula mixture.

Persian Baked Stuffed Fish (Mahi Shekam Por with Shivid Polo)

Do you have the memory of a certain aroma from a childhood dinner? *Mahi Shekam Por* was a specialty of my Persian grandmother and I think of her when I make this dish. She typically served it with dilled rice (*Shivid Polo*). We would follow our noses to the kitchen to watch the crispy fish come from the oven. Later I learned the magic that herbs, walnuts and pomegranate molasses do for this sweet and delicate fish, and I have created a keto-friendly *Shivid Polo* to accompany the *Mahi Shekam Por*. Welcome to my grandmother's kitchen!

Serves 6   Total carbs: 11 g   Net carbs: 7 g   Fat: 26 g   Protein: 35 g

---

Fish

1 tsp turmeric

1 tsp salt

1 tsp pepper

1 tsp seafood seasoning

2 whole medium-sized fish such as trout, branzino or red snapper (2.2 lb [1 kg] each)

Juice of 1 lemon

Filling

2 tbsp (30 ml) olive oil

1 yellow onion, diced

3 cloves garlic, chopped

1 cup (60 g) fresh cilantro, chopped

¾ cup (112 g) walnuts, chopped

¼ cup (30 g) sugar-free dried cranberries

1 tsp lime juice

1 tbsp (15 ml) pomegranate molasses

2 tbsp (25 g) granulated allulose

1 tsp salt

1 tsp black pepper

Line a rimmed baking sheet with parchment paper.

To prepare the fish, combine the turmeric, salt, pepper and seafood seasoning in a small bowl.

Rinse the fish with cold water. Use paper towels to pat them dry. Rub the fish inside and out with the spice mixture and lemon juice.

To prepare the filling, heat the oil in a large skillet over medium heat. Add the onion and garlic and sauté for 7 minutes, then add the cilantro, walnuts, cranberries, lime juice, pomegranate molasses, granulated allulose, salt and pepper to form a stuffing; cook the mixture for 5 minutes, stirring, then remove it from the heat and let it cool.

Preheat the oven to 400°F (200°C).

Fill the inside of the fish with all of the cooled stuffing, then use kitchen twine to tie the fish closed near the front and tail ends.

(continued)

Persian Baked Stuffed Fish
(*Mahi Shekam Por* with *Shivid Polo*) (**cont.**)

Glaze

¼ tsp saffron, ground

2 tbsp (30 ml) hot water

2 tbsp (28 g) salted butter, melted

Dill Rice

2 tbsp (30 g) ghee, coconut oil or extra virgin olive oil

1 clove garlic, minced

5 cups (500 g) cauliflower rice

1 tbsp (15 ml) white vinegar

1 tbsp (15 ml) fresh lemon juice

¼ cup (15 g) fresh dill, chopped, or 3 tbsp (9 g) dried dill

½ tsp sea salt, or to taste

¼ tsp black pepper, or to taste

To make the saffron glaze, dissolve the saffron in the hot water, then add the melted butter. Brush the outside of the fish with the saffron butter glaze and place the pan on the center rack in the oven. Bake the fish for 30 to 40 minutes, until it flakes easily with a fork. Be sure to glaze the fish one more time during the baking process.

While the fish cooks, make the dill rice. Grease a large saucepan with ghee and add the minced garlic. Mix it and cook over medium heat for 1 minute. Add the riced cauliflower, white vinegar and lemon juice and cook it for 12 to 15 minutes, stirring frequently. Add the fresh dill. Season it with salt and pepper and mix well.

Remove the fish from the oven, allowing it to sit for 5 minutes before removing the twine. Serve the fish with the dill rice.

BBQ Chicken Pizza

Do you ever crave a spicy pizza? This keto version is ideal for sharing with family and friends and it will absolutely pass the taste test for flavor, texture and goodness! My homemade barbecue sauce is excellent, but you can use a purchased sauce if you desire. There's lots of flavor for everyone on this pizza, and the crust is just right. Pick a movie, make this pizza and enjoy a family night in!

Serves 9   Total carbs: 12 g   Net carbs: 7 g   Fat: 19 g   Protein: 38 g

---

BBQ Sauce

1½ cups (337 g) tomato paste

2 tbsp (25 g) brown sweetener

¼ cup (50 g) allulose sweetener

2 tbsp (30 ml) Worcestershire sauce

4 tbsp (60 ml) apple cider vinegar

1 dash hot pepper sauce

½ tsp smoked paprika

1 tsp garlic powder

¼ tsp mustard powder

¼ tsp salt

1 cup (235 ml) water

BBQ Chicken

½ tsp smoked paprika

¼ tsp garlic powder

⅛ tsp salt

⅛ tsp pepper

8 oz (227 g) skinless chicken tenderloins

½ tbsp (7 ml) avocado oil

¼ cup (58 ml) BBQ sauce (see above or use store bought)

Make the BBQ sauce if you're not using a store-bought version. In a small saucepan over medium heat, stir together the tomato paste, brown sweetener, allulose, Worcestershire sauce, apple cider vinegar, hot pepper sauce, smoked paprika, garlic powder, mustard powder and salt. Bring it to a simmer, then remove it from the heat and add the water. Bring the sauce to a gentle boil over medium-high heat, then reduce the heat to medium low. Simmer, stirring frequently, for 20 minutes, or until slightly thickened. Allow the sauce to cool slightly before using it.

While the sauce cooks, prepare the chicken. In a small bowl, combine the smoked paprika, garlic powder, salt and pepper. Season both sides of the chicken with the spices.

Heat a skillet over medium heat. Add the avocado oil and swirl to coat the surface of the skillet. Add the seasoned chicken tenderloins and cook for 5 to 7 minutes on each side, or until cooked through (internal temperature of 165°F [74°C]). Transfer the chicken to a clean cutting board.

Let the chicken rest for about 5 minutes, then chop it into small pieces. Add ¼ cup (58 ml) of BBQ sauce to the chopped chicken and stir to coat the chicken in the sauce.

(continued)

BBQ **Chicken Pizza (cont.)**

Pizza

1 batch Versatile Naan dough (page 59)

Olive oil, for brushing

$\frac{1}{4}$ cup (58 ml) BBQ sauce (see page 33 or use store bought)

1 cup (225 g) Monterey Jack cheese, shredded

1 cup (113 g) shredded mozzarella cheese

1 jalapeño, sliced (optional)

$\frac{1}{4}$ cup (13 g) sliced red onion

2 tbsp (4 g) fresh cilantro, chopped, for garnish

Preheat the oven to 450°F (232°C). Place a pizza stone or heavy baking sheet in the oven, keeping it in the oven while it heats so it is very hot when you are ready to cook the pizza.

Roll the dough out to a size that fits on the prepared pan. Brush the dough lightly with olive oil, making sure to coat the edges. Carefully remove the pizza stone from the oven. Arrange the dough on the pizza stone. Bake the pizza for 5 minutes.

Carefully spread about $\frac{1}{4}$ cup (58 ml) of BBQ sauce over the partially cooked dough. Add the Monterey Jack cheese, shredded mozzarella cheese, BBQ chicken, sliced jalapeño (if using) and sliced onion to the pizza. Bake the pizza for 10 to 12 minutes, or until the crust and cheeses are golden brown. Garnish the pizza with cilantro, slice it and serve.

Spectacular Spiral Meat Roll (*Borek*)

Many cultures have savory pastries; this Middle Eastern dish originated
in Turkey and stands out in taste and unique appearance. This meat-filled
version of *Borek* is a keto variation that will have your family and guests
thinking they are visiting an exotic locale. The herbs and spices are very
subtle, but the spectacular effect of the tasty meat filling in the golden
coiled pastry is unforgettable. *Afiyet olsun*! Enjoy your meal!

Serves 8   Total carbs: 10 g   Net carbs: 5 g   Fat: 27 g   Protein: 34 g

---

½ cup (26 g) finely chopped onion

½ lb (227 g) ground beef chuck (or a combination of beef, pork and/or lamb)

2 tbsp (30 ml) avocado oil

¼ cup (37 g) chopped green bell pepper

1 tbsp (17 g) salt

1 tsp pepper

½ tsp turmeric (optional)

1 tbsp (14 g) tomato paste

¼ cup (15 g) fresh parsley, chopped

1 batch Versatile Naan dough (page 59)

1 cup (113 g) shredded Gouda cheese

¼ cup (56 g) salted butter, melted

1 egg, lightly beaten with 1 tsp water, for egg wash

1 tbsp (9 g) sesame seeds

In a large skillet, sauté the onion and ground meat over medium heat until the meat is no longer pink and the onion is translucent, about 5 minutes. Drain the meat and onion in a colander. Return the meat and onion mixture to the skillet and add the avocado oil, green bell pepper, salt, pepper and turmeric (if using) and cook for 2 minutes. Add the tomato paste and stir until it is mixed thoroughly. Cover it with a lid and let the meat cook for 5 more minutes, then remove the lid and add the parsley. Remove the mixture from the heat and let it cool to room temperature.

Preheat the oven to 375°F (190°C) and grease an ovenproof skillet or pie plate.

Divide the dough into four pieces and roll each piece with a rolling pin into a 10 x 2.5–inch (25 x 6–cm) rectangle. Spread one-quarter of the Gouda cheese down the long side of the dough and spoon one-quarter of the meat mixture on top of the cheese. Firmly roll the filled dough into a long log. Starting with one end, form a flat coiled spiral from the tube of dough. Place the spiral into the center of the greased baking dish.

Make another meat tube and place its end against the end of the first tube in the pan, continuing the spiral. Form and spiral the other meat tubes until the whole skillet is covered. Brush the large spiral of dough with melted butter, then brush it with the egg wash and sprinkle it with the sesame seeds.

Bake the meat roll for 20 to 30 minutes, or until the dough is golden brown.

Store, covered, in the refrigerator for up to 5 days.

Aromatic **Green Bean Rice (*Lubia Polo*)**

This is a satisfying dish that is a delight to the senses! Fragrant spices warm the sauce that is the base for a hearty mélange of flavors. It's so intriguing that no one will notice that the rice is actually tasty cauliflower.

Serves 4   Total carbs: 10.2   Net carbs: 6.4 g   Fat: 22 g   Protein: 16 g

Meatballs

1 lb (454 g) ground beef

1 tsp turmeric

1 tsp sea salt

½ tsp cayenne pepper, or to taste

2 tbsp (30 ml) virgin avocado oil or olive oil, for frying

Cauliflower Rice and Green Beans

3 cups (300 g) green beans

½ tsp saffron

¼ cup (60 ml) boiling water

1 small yellow onion, chopped

2 cloves garlic, chopped

1 tbsp (14 g) salted butter or ghee

1 tsp cinnamon

1 tsp curry powder

2 tbsp (30 g) tomato paste

1 tbsp (15 ml) lemon juice

4 cups (400 g) cauliflower rice

1 tbsp (15 ml) white wine vinegar

Sea salt and pepper, to taste

For the meatballs, combine the ground beef, turmeric, sea salt and cayenne pepper in a bowl. Using your hands, make 20 to 25 small meatballs, ¾ inch (2 cm) in diameter. Fry the meatballs in a large frying pan greased with avocado oil over medium heat. Cook for 2 minutes and then turn until they are cooked on all sides. Transfer the meatballs to a plate and set them aside.

For the cauliflower rice and green beans, cut the green beans into 1-inch (2.5-cm) pieces.

Meanwhile, prepare the saffron in a small bowl by adding the boiling water. Set it aside to soak while you prepare the sauce.

In a large pan, sauté the onion and garlic in the butter until they are golden brown. Add the cinnamon, curry powder, tomato paste and lemon juice. Mix well until everything is combined and cook it for 2 to 3 minutes.

Stir in the green beans and saffron water and bring the sauce to a low simmer. Cover and cook it until the green beans are crisp tender, for 10 to 12 minutes. At this point, return the meatballs to the pan.

While the green beans are cooking, microwave the cauliflower rice in a heatproof bowl for 6 minutes until softened.

Add the cooked cauliflower and the vinegar to the pan and stir to blend them with the green beans, meatballs and sauce. Season with salt and pepper to taste.

Serve immediately or let it cool down and store it in the fridge for up to 4 days.

Persian Meatballs (*Koofteh*)

When I was a little girl, I always loved the day my mother made *Koofteh*, when I helped her smash the walnuts and peel the hard-boiled eggs. There was always a secret hiding inside each delicious large beef or lamb meatball that was subtly spiced and simmered in a light tomato-flavored sauce. The treasure is a hidden hard-boiled egg, surrounded by dried fruit and nuts, on the inside of this classic Persian dish. And thanks to the cauliflower rice, it's keto!

Serves 4   Total carbs: 12 g   Net carbs: 9 g   Fat: 37 g   Protein: 42 g

---

Meatball Filling

4 eggs

1 tbsp (8 g) dried cranberries or barberries, rinsed, divided

4 tbsp (29 g) walnut pieces, chopped, divided

Sauce

2 tbsp (30 ml) olive oil, for frying

1 large onion, thinly sliced

3 cloves garlic, peeled and chopped

2 tbsp (28 g) tomato paste

1 tsp salt

1 tsp black pepper

1 tsp ground turmeric

5 cups (1.2 L) water

1 tbsp (15 ml) fresh lemon juice

Begin by hard boiling the eggs by cooking them in boiling water for 10 minutes. Let them cool, then peel off the shells and set them aside.

Next, start making the sauce. In a large Dutch oven, heat the olive oil over medium heat and brown the onion and garlic for about 5 minutes Add the tomato paste and sauté for 1 more minute, then add the salt, pepper, turmeric, water and lemon juice. Bring it to a boil, then reduce the heat to low and allow the sauce to simmer while you make the meatballs.

(continued)

Meatballs

1 cup (124 g) cauliflower rice

1 small onion

2 tbsp (20 g) hemp seeds, rinsed

1 lb (454 g) ground beef or lamb

2 tbsp (13 g) almond flour

1 tsp saffron, ground and dissolved in 1 tbsp (15 ml) hot water

¼ cup (24 g) fresh tarragon, chopped, or 2 tsp (5 g) dried tarragon

¼ cup (15 g) fresh parsley, chopped, or 2 tsp (5 g) dried parsley

¼ cup (6 g) chopped fresh mint or ½ tsp dried mint

1 tsp turmeric

1½ tsp (9 g) salt

1 tsp black pepper

1 tsp ground cumin

1 tsp cinnamon

1 large egg

1 tsp mayonnaise

Prepare the cauliflower rice for the meatballs by microwaving the riced cauliflower for 4 minutes, then drain the water. Let it cool. Next, grate the onion. Put the onion into a sieve placed over a bowl and use a spoon to press and drain the juice, or use a cheesecloth and squeeze to drain the liquid completely. (Reserve the juice to use later while forming the meatballs.)

In a wide mixing bowl, combine the grated onion, cauliflower rice, hemp seeds, ground beef, almond flour, saffron water, fresh tarragon, fresh parsley, fresh mint, turmeric, salt, pepper, cumin and cinnamon in a bowl and knead the mixture by hand (or use a stand mixer) for 1 minute. Add the egg and mayonnaise and continue to knead for about 5 minutes longer, until the mixture is sticky and holds its shape when it is rolled into a ball. Cover the meat mixture and allow it to rest in the refrigerator for at least 30 minutes and up to 24 hours.

Now the fun part, making the meatballs! Divide the meat mixture into four portions. Place the bowl of onion juice next to you. Wet your hands with the onion juice and roll each portion of the mixture into a ball the size of an orange. Use your fingers to make a deep, wide hole in the center of the ball. Place ¼ tablespoon of cranberries and 1 tablespoon (7 g) of chopped walnuts into the hole, then insert one peeled hard-boiled egg. Close up the hole with meat paste and shape a large, smooth ball. Repeat for the remaining meat mixture and eggs.

Drop one meatball into the sauce and wait for the sauce to return to a gentle boil before dropping in the next meatball. Repeat with the remaining meatballs. Cook the meatballs uncovered for 25 minutes after all the meatballs are in the sauce, then cover and turn the heat down to low.

Simmer the meatballs for at least 1 hour without moving the meatballs. Continue cooking if the sauce is too thin. When the sauce has thickened to your liking, adjust the seasoning to taste and simmer for a few more minutes. Enjoy!

Tahcheen Baked Saffron Rice Cake with Chicken

Classic recipes like *Tahcheen-e-Morgh* are almost sacred in the culture where they were developed, and my Baked Saffron Rice Cake with Chicken is no exception. The traditional recipe features fragrant, crispy Basmati rice cooked in a timeless way. *Tahcheen* means "arranged on the bottom" and refers to the special technique of cooking the rice long and slowly in the bottom of the pot and turning out the rice cake onto a plate so that the crispy part is visible. In this low-carb version, you will find a very satisfying base of marinated cauliflower rice, seasoned to perfection with saffron, orange peel and yogurt. Like the classic, it is crunchy on the outside and soft and flavorful on the inside.

The *Morgh* (chicken) is equally delicious! Cooking chicken thighs slowly on a bed of caramelized onions with smoky spices yields a delicious melt-in-your-mouth taste. Don't rush this step because it is the key to the complex flavors expected in this dish. It's a technique you'll want to know for other chicken dishes too. You won't want to miss a morsel of this tasty keto masterpiece!

Serves 6   Total carbs: 10 g   Net carbs: 6 g   Fat: 20 g   Protein: 34 g

---

Chicken
2 tsp (6 g) smoked paprika

2 tsp (6 g) turmeric

2 tsp (7 g) garlic powder

Salt and pepper, to taste

1 medium onion, thinly sliced

1 lb (454 g) boneless chicken thighs

½ tsp saffron, ground and dissolved in 1 tbsp (15 ml) hot water

2 tbsp (28 g) salted butter

1 tbsp (15 ml) lemon juice

To prepare the chicken, mix the paprika, turmeric, garlic powder, salt and pepper until combined. In a large frying pan, add the onion in a single layer, then top them with half of the spice mixture. Place the chicken over the onion, sprinkling it with the remaining spice mixture.

Add the saffron water on top. Cut the butter into small pieces and arrange them on top of the chicken and spices, then add the lemon juice. Cover it with a lid and let the chicken cook over medium heat for 20 minutes. Then flip all the chicken pieces and let them cook for another 25 minutes. Shred the chicken when it is cool enough to handle and set it aside.

(continued)

Rice Mixture

1 cup (235 ml) full fat Greek yogurt

⅓ cup (79 ml) sour cream

2 tbsp (30 ml) avocado oil

3 egg yolks

½ tsp saffron with 4 tbsp (60 ml) water

Pinch of salt and pepper

6 cups (600 g) frozen cauliflower rice

4 tbsp (58 g) salted butter, melted, divided

Topping (Optional)

½ tbsp (7 ml) avocado oil

3 tbsp (21 g) dried barberries

1 tbsp (14 g) granulated erythritol

¼ tsp saffron, ground and dissolved in 1 tbsp (15 ml) rose water

½ tbsp (7 ml) fresh lemon juice

3 tbsp (28 g) slivered pistachios

To prepare the cauliflower rice, in a medium bowl, place the yogurt, sour cream, avocado oil, egg yolks, saffron water, salt and pepper, then add the frozen cauliflower rice to the mixture and combine them.

Preheat the oven to 400°F (200°C). Grease a nonstick, ovenproof 8-inch (20-cm) pot with 2 tablespoons (30 ml) of the melted butter.

Lay some of the marinade-coated cauliflower rice on the bottom of the pot and press the rice up the sides of the pot by 1½ inches (4 cm). Distribute the chicken pieces over the cauliflower, then top with the remaining cauliflower. Drizzle the remaining melted butter over the top layer. Depending on the size of your pot, you can repeat these layers, finishing with the cauliflower mixture.

Bake the Tahcheen for 45 minutes, or until the top is golden. Let it rest in the pan for 5 minutes. Place a large plate or platter over the pot and invert the two so the Tahcheen falls onto the plate.

To prepare the topping (optional), in a small skillet, add the avocado oil, barberries, granulated erythritol, saffron water and lemon juice and stir-fry over medium heat for 2 minutes. Add the slivered pistachios and remove from the heat, adding it to the Tahcheen just before serving.

Super Juicy Chicken Paprikash

Hungarians love their chicken paprikash, and it's such an easy dish to make that it will become one of your go-to dinners too. A few keto secrets are hiding among the flavors to give this an authentic taste and thickness, and everyone agrees that this chicken paprikash is a winner! Enjoy with cauliflower rice to complete your meal.

Serves 6   Total carbs: 6 g   Net carbs: 5 g   Fat: 22 g   Protein: 47 g

---

4 tbsp (60 ml) olive oil

2.2 lb (1 kg) chicken (12 drumsticks and thighs)

1 large onion, chopped

3 cloves garlic, peeled and minced

½ cup (100 g) tomato, chopped (1 tomato)

½ cup (74 g) chopped green bell pepper

3 tbsp (20 g) Hungarian paprika, sweet or hot or a combination

1 tsp salt, plus more to taste

¼ tsp black pepper, plus more to taste

1 cup (237 ml) chicken stock

1 tbsp (8 g) arrowroot flour

1 tsp xanthan gum

¼ cup (60 ml) heavy whipping cream

½ cup (123 ml) sour cream

Heat a heavy-bottomed pot over medium heat until it is hot. Add the olive oil and swirl to coat the bottom of the pot. When the oil is hot, add the chicken and brown each piece on all sides. Transfer the chicken to a plate. In the same oil, add the onion and fry it until it is golden brown, about 7 minutes. Add the garlic, tomato and green bell pepper and fry them for another 2 to 3 minutes. Remove the pot from the heat and stir in the paprika, salt and pepper (paprika becomes bitter if scorched).

Return the chicken to the pot and place it back over the heat. Pour in the chicken stock. The chicken should be mostly covered. Bring it to a boil. Cover the pot, reduce the heat to medium low and simmer for 40 minutes. Remove the chicken and transfer to a plate.

In a small bowl, stir the arrowroot flour, xanthan gum, heavy whipping cream and sour cream together to form a smooth paste. Stir the cream mixture into the sauce, whisking constantly to prevent lumps. Bring it to a simmer for a couple of minutes until the sauce is thickened. Add salt and pepper to taste. Return the chicken to the sauce and simmer to heat through. Enjoy!

Store in a covered container in the refrigerator for up to 5 days.

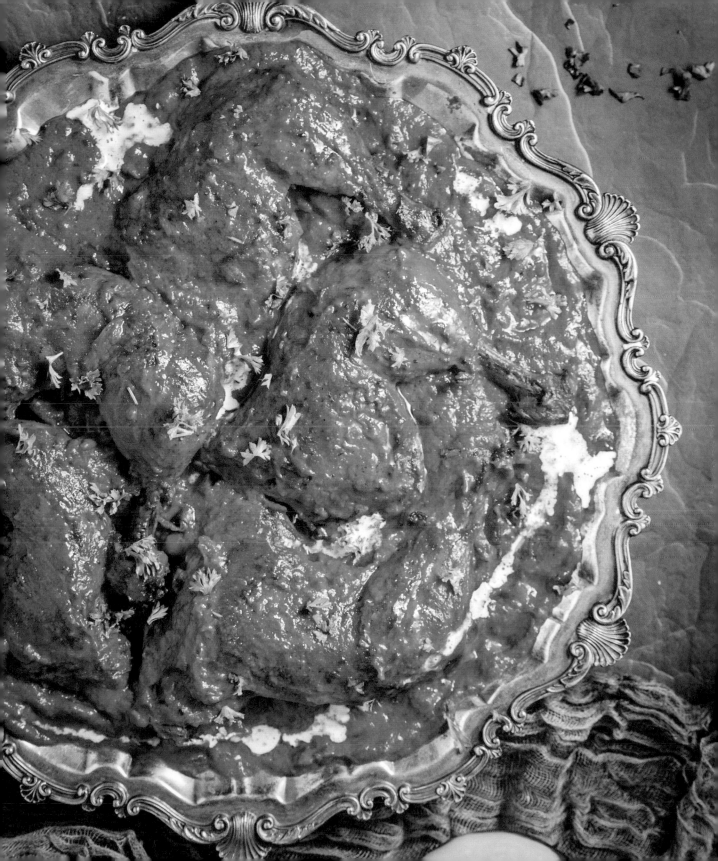

Kaveh's Chicken Biryani

Chicken Biryani is a special request at our house. In my version, cauliflower rice plays a tasty supporting role to the spicy chicken and sweet caramelized onions that form the traditional layers of this classic dish from India.

Serves 6   Total carbs: 4 g   Net carbs: 3 g   Fat: 18 g   Protein: 30 g

Chicken

¼ cup (60 ml) full fat Greek-style yogurt

1 tsp garam masala

½ tsp ground turmeric

½ tsp ground coriander

¼ tsp ground cumin

¼ tsp red chili flakes

1 tbsp (15 ml) lime juice

½ tsp salt

2.2 lb (1 kg) bone-in, skinless chicken thighs

1 tbsp (15 g) ghee or avocado oil

1 cup (240 ml) chicken broth

Rice

2 tbsp (30 g) ghee, divided

1 red onion, thinly sliced

1 tsp minced garlic

1 tsp minced ginger

1 jalapeño, seeded and chopped

¼ cup (4 g) mint, chopped

½ cup (8 g) fresh cilantro, chopped, plus more for serving

¼ tsp saffron, ground and dissolved in 2 tbsp (30 ml) boiling water

6 cups (600 g) riced cauliflower

Kosher salt, to taste

Chopped cilantro, for garnish (optional)

To prepare the chicken for the biryani, combine the yogurt, garam masala, turmeric, coriander, cumin, chili flakes, lime juice and salt in a large bowl and stir them together. Add the chicken pieces and toss them together, making sure the chicken is thoroughly coated in the marinade. Allow the chicken to marinate for at least 1 hour or overnight.

Heat a large, deep skillet over medium-high heat.

Melt the ghee in the skillet, add the chicken and cook it until it is browned on both sides. Add the chicken broth, cover and let it cook for 20 minutes.

To prepare the rice, in another skillet over medium heat, add 1 tablespoon (15 g) of ghee and sauté the onion until it is well caramelized, 15 to 20 minutes. Transfer the caramelized onion to a bowl and set it aside.

Grease a large saucepan with 1 tablespoon (15 g) of ghee and add the minced garlic, ginger, chopped jalapeño, mint and cilantro. Mix and cook over medium-low heat for up to 1 minute and set aside.

To assemble the biryani, add the saffron water to the cauliflower rice and toss to distribute it evenly. Next, add the mixture of garlic, ginger, jalapeño, mint and cilantro with the salt to the cauliflower rice and mix it well. Add half the seasoned cauliflower mixture to the bottom of a deep pot. Top the cauliflower rice with the chicken in a single layer. Top the chicken with an even layer of caramelized onions.

Finish assembling the biryani by adding the rest of the cauliflower rice in an even layer. Cover the pot with a lid and put the pot on the stove over medium heat, setting the timer for 20 minutes. Mix the chicken biryani together and then transfer it to a serving platter. Garnish with fresh cilantro (if using) and serve.

Savory Mushroom Galette

Pie for dinner? Yes, please! Hearty cremini mushrooms, fresh herbs and several cheeses give the peek-a-boo filling lots of flavor and texture in this rustic pie. Keto-perfect pastry dough makes an attractive case and helps limit carbs. This dish is beautiful and delicious, and who would think this was a keto recipe?

Serves 8   **Total carbs: 12 g**   **Net carbs: 4 g**   **Fat: 25 g**   **Protein: 18 g**

---

1 tbsp (15 ml) olive oil

½ white onion, thinly sliced

1½ lb (680 g) cremini mushrooms, cut into slices

2 tbsp (28 g) unsalted butter

Pinch of salt and freshly ground pepper

2 eggs, 1 beaten, for egg wash

1 tsp whole milk

1 sheet Leili's Perfect Pastry Dough (page 68)

1 cup (250 g) whole milk ricotta cheese

¼ cup (23 g) grated Parmesan cheese

¼ tsp salt

1 clove garlic, finely minced

Pinch of nutmeg

1.5 oz (42 g) Gruyère cheese, shredded

1 tsp fresh thyme, chopped

1 tsp fresh rosemary, chopped

1 tsp fresh sage, chopped

Sesame seeds, for garnish (optional)

Preheat the oven to 375°F (190°C). Line a large baking sheet with parchment paper.

Heat the olive oil in a large pan and, once it is hot, add in the onion slices. Cook them over medium heat until the onions begin to become golden along the edges and caramelize, about 7 minutes.

Add the mushroom slices to the pan with the butter and cook for another few minutes until the mushrooms are tender. Season them lightly with salt and pepper. Turn off the heat and set the pan aside. Allow the mixture to cool to room temperature before assembling the galette. Meanwhile, whisk together the beaten egg and milk in a small bowl. Set it aside.

On a floured work surface, roll the dough into a 15-inch (38-cm) circle, about ¼ inch (6 mm) thick. Transfer to the lined baking sheet. Mix the ricotta cheese with the Parmesan, 1 egg, salt, garlic and nutmeg. Spread the ricotta mixture on the dough, leaving a 2-inch (5-cm) border.

Distribute the mushroom and onion mixture all over the ricotta cheese, then top that with the shredded Gruyère. Sprinkle it with the chopped thyme, rosemary and sage. Using the unfilled edge, fold the pastry up over the filling, pleating every 2 inches (5 cm). The center of the filling will be visible, as is traditional in a galette. Lightly brush the edges of the dough with the egg wash.

Bake the galette for 20 to 30 minutes. Let the galette rest for 10 minutes on the baking sheet, then garnish with sesame seeds (if using) and transfer it to your serving plate.

Georgian **Cheesy Bread (*Khachapouri*)**

What looks like a canoe, bubbles in the oven and is fun to eat? *Khachapouri!*
In the country of Georgia, this traditional food has a few variations among
cooks, but all involve a floury crust, a coating of cheese and a runny egg on the
top. My Versatile Naan dough is the keto secret to this lightly spiced meat pie.
Call your family and guests to break off a piece and try the melting goodness.
Of course, it can also be eaten with a fork!

Serves 6   Total carbs: 9 g   Net carbs: 6 g   Fat: 29 g   Protein: 44 g

---

1 lb (454 g) ground lamb or
beef

2 tbsp (30 ml) olive oil

1 onion, chopped

2 tbsp (28 g) tomato paste

2 cloves garlic, chopped

1 tsp paprika

¼ cup (8 g) fresh mint,
chopped

Salt and pepper, to taste

1 batch Versatile Naan dough
(page 59)

2 tbsp (15 g) oat fiber, for
rolling dough

1 cup (113 g) grated Cheddar
cheese, divided

1 egg, beaten, for egg wash

2 large eggs, for filling

1 tbsp (2 g) fresh parsley,
chopped

Sesame seeds, for garnish
(optional)

Preheat the oven to 350°F (177°C). Line a baking tray with a baking mat
or parchment paper.

Heat a large skillet over medium heat. Add the meat to the hot skillet with
the olive oil and brown it for about 5 minutes. Add the onion, tomato paste,
garlic, paprika, mint, salt and pepper. Simmer for another 10 minutes. Set
it aside and let it cool.

Divide the Versatile Naan dough into two parts. This way you will end up
with two large khachapouri. Using a rolling pin, roll the dough out into a
circular shape, ⅛ inch (3 mm) thick.

Dust the surface of the baking sheet with a little oat fiber to prevent the
moisture of the fillings from soaking through the dough. Place the dough
on the baking sheet and form an oval shape.

Sprinkle half of the Cheddar cheese over the dough, leaving a
1-inch (2.5-cm) border around the edge. Roll one side of the circle
toward the center, then repeat with the opposite side so that the edges
of the dough make a boat shape. Pinch the open ends of the dough
together on both sides and twist them together to form the two pointed
ends of the boat shape. Leave a gap of about 4 inches (10 cm) between
the two khachapouri on the tray.

Place the cooled meat mixture on top of the cheese on the dough. Using a
pastry brush, brush the sides of the khachapouri with the beaten egg. Bake
the khachapouri for 20 minutes.

Remove the pan from the oven and pour a large egg on top of the meat
of each khachapouri, centered. Add the remaining grated cheese and
return the pan to the oven for another 10 minutes, or until it's golden
brown. Sprinkle the fresh parsley on top, garnish with sesame seeds
(if using) and enjoy!

Bake from
the Heart

These bread recipes are my babies, the ones that I worked the hardest to perfect. Because a good bread can add so much satisfaction to a meal and a disappointing bread can make you feel deprived, I felt it was important to make these bread recipes one of the foundations of the cookbook. These are not "nutty" breads as you will find in some keto sources. They are not "fathead" breads as some make. These are actual breads that emulate the breads you crave.

You'll find a variety of keto flour substitutions in these recipes, but there are some other ingredients that will make your breads successful: temperature, patience and passion. Yeast is the prima donna, but once she is satisfied, she is happy to do a wonderful job. So keep the temperature slightly warm and constant, allow enough time for the dough to rise before you go to the next step and use these delicious keto breads to round out your meals. These are the breads we eat in my house when we want pasta or sandwiches, the basic building blocks of family meals. They've been a hit with my guests too, who assume there will only be salad on the menu but are pleasantly surprised.

I've included some tips for successful bread baking in the Bread Baking Tips section on page 169, and you can learn more about some of the ingredients in this chapter that you may or may not be familiar with in The Keto Pantry: Ingredients and Tools section on page 166.

Keep some of these recipes up your sleeve and enjoy the variety they add to your meals. Expect some compliments!

Lovin' **Loaf (Bread)**

Whenever someone hears about keto and low-carb diets, the first thing that comes to mind is obviously "How about bread?! I love bread and I can't give it up!"

Good news! There are plenty of keto-friendly flour substitutes that we can use instead of normal flours for cooking bread in a keto way. There are some adjustments needed because the flours work differently from wheat flours and may differ in taste and texture. This recipe, however, gives you a loaf that you can serve proudly and confidently because I've done the hard part. Don't worry, the sugar used to activate the yeast is consumed by the yeast. For a more traditional flavor, stir in the optional wheat-flavored extract.

Makes 12 slices   Total carbs: 7 g   Net carbs: 2 g   Fat: 5 g   Protein: 12 g

---

1¼ cups (150 g) vital wheat gluten

½ cup (45 g) oat fiber

¼ cup (37 g) flaxseed meal

⅓ cup (32 g) lupin flour

1 tsp salt

2 tbsp (29 g) heavy cream powder

1 tsp dough conditioner or 1 tsp xanthan gum

2 tbsp (25 g) powdered erythritol

1 tbsp (8 g) active dry or instant yeast

1 cup (235 ml) warm water (100–110°F [43–49°C])

1 tbsp (12 g) honey, sugar or maple syrup (to feed the yeast)

2 tbsp (28.5 g) organic shortening (or 2 tbsp [28 g] softened, salted butter)

2 eggs, lightly beaten

10 drops wheat-flavored extract (optional)

In a medium bowl whisk the vital wheat gluten, oat fiber, flaxseed meal, lupin flour, salt, heavy cream powder, dough conditioner and powdered erythritol together. Set the bowl aside.

If you're using active dry yeast, activate the yeast by combining it with the warm water and 1 tablespoon (12 g) of honey in a 4-quart (4-L) mixing bowl (or stand mixer bowl with the paddle attachment). Give the mixture a quick stir and let rest until the yeast appears foamy on the surface, about 5 minutes.

If using rapid rise instant yeast, simply combine the yeast with the warm water and honey, sugar or maple syrup, give them a quick stir and move on to the next step.

Add the organic shortening, beaten eggs and wheat-flavored extract (if using) to the yeast mixture. Whisk them together for 30 seconds. Pour in the flour mixture and mix until a dough forms. Switch from the paddle attachment to the dough hook and, on medium speed, knead for 7 minutes (or knead with your hands on a lightly floured surface for 10 minutes).

For the first rise, lightly grease a large bowl with cooking spray and place the dough in it, turning to coat all the surfaces. Cover the bowl with a dish towel or plastic wrap and allow the dough to rise in a warm place (see Tips) until doubled in size, about 1½ hours. Punch the dough down well to remove the air bubbles. Shape the ball into a long log and place it into a 9 x 5–inch (23 x 13–cm) loaf pan (see Tips).

(continued)

Lovin' **Loaf (Bread) (cont.)**

Cooking spray

1 egg white and 1 tbsp (15 ml) water, for egg wash (optional)

1 tbsp (14 g) salted butter, melted

For the second rise, spray one piece of plastic wrap with cooking spray and lay it gently over the dough in the pan. Allow the dough to rise again for about 30 minutes, then gently remove the covering.

Preheat the oven to 375°F (190°C) toward the end of the second rise. Brush the top of the loaf with the egg white wash (if using) and bake the bread for 30 to 33 minutes, loosely covering it with aluminum foil for the last 15 minutes.

Transfer the loaf from the loaf pan to a wire cooling rack. Brush the top with the butter and allow it cool for at least 10 minutes before slicing.

Once cool, store the loaf in an airtight container or bag for 2 to 3 days at room temperature, or up to 5 days in the refrigerator.

Tips: To speed up the rising time of the first rise, place the dough into a well-greased bowl and turn it once to grease the dough all over. Cover the bowl with plastic wrap. Preheat the oven to 180°F (82°C), then turn the oven off. Place the bowl into the oven, leaving the oven door slightly cracked open. Allow the dough to rise until it is doubled, then remove it from the bowl, punch it down and shape it into a loaf.

Wondering how to make bread without a loaf pan? If you've got a skillet, baking sheet, casserole dish or cake pan, you can still bake bread at home. Form the dough into a ball after the first rise and allow it to rise the second time on the greased baking sheet or skillet as you prefer. The baking time will be similar, but be sure to test for doneness.

Versatile Naan

Nothing says *home* like the smell of baking! Here's the "scoop" you need to make bread that can be used for scooping food, holding meat for tacos or making pizza crust. Of course, it's great with Kaveh's Chicken Biryani (page 49) and other dishes.

If you are a baker, you will find the ingredients somewhat different from conventional recipes to account for the low carbs. (And by the way, the yeast will consume the extra carbs used to activate it, so your carb count won't be affected.) After testing this recipe many times, I can assure you that it will work perfectly for you and be a delicious addition to your meals. This is a good recipe for a beginner baker. Just follow my directions and give it a try!

I've included steps for an optional garlic/herb butter topping for a nice variation.

Serves 6   Total carbs: 8 g   Net carbs: 4 g   Fat: 10 g   Protein: 23 g

---

1 cup (120 g) vital wheat gluten

¼ cup (25 g) almond flour

½ cup (25 g) lupin flour

1 tsp salt

2 tbsp (29 g) heavy cream powder

1 tsp dough conditioner

1 tbsp (4 g) wheat protein isolate 5000

1 tbsp (4 g) oat fiber

1 tsp baking powder

2 tbsp (25 g) powdered erythritol

2½ tsp (4 g) active dry or instant yeast

½ cup (120 ml) warm water (100–110°F [38–43°C])

1 tbsp (12 g) honey, sugar or maple syrup (to feed the yeast)

2 tbsp (28 g) organic shortening (or 2 tbsp [28 g] softened salted butter)

1 egg, lightly beaten

10 drops wheat-flavored extract (optional)

In a medium bowl, whisk the vital wheat gluten, almond flour, lupin flour, salt, heavy cream powder, dough conditioner, wheat protein isolate 5000, oat fiber, baking powder and powdered erythritol. Set the bowl aside.

If you're using active dry yeast, activate the yeast by combining it with the warm water and 1 tablespoon (12 g) of honey in a 4-quart (4-L) mixing bowl (or stand mixer with the paddle attachment). Give the mixture a quick stir and let this rest until the yeast appears foamy on the surface, about 5 minutes.

If you're using rapid rise instant yeast, no activation is needed. Simply combine the yeast with the warm water and honey, sugar or maple syrup, give them a quick stir and move on to the next step.

Add the organic shortening, beaten egg and wheat-flavored extract (if using) to the yeast mixture. Whisk them for 30 seconds. Pour the flour mixture into the bowl and mix until a dough forms. Switch from the paddle attachment to the dough hook and mix on medium speed, kneading for 7 minutes.

(continued)

Cooking spray

2 tbsp (30 g) ghee or salted butter, for brushing

1 clove garlic, minced, for garlic butter (optional)

1 tbsp (2 g) fresh parsley or cilantro, chopped, for garlic butter (optional)

2 tbsp (14 g) oat fiber, for dusting and flouring

Remove the dough from the mixing bowl and use your hands to shape it into a ball. Grease the mixing bowl (or a separate bowl) lightly with cooking spray, then place the dough ball back in the bowl and lightly cover it with plastic wrap sprayed with cooking spray. Place the bowl in a warm location and let the dough rise for 2 hours, or until the dough has nearly doubled in size.

During the last 10 minutes of the dough's rising time, heat the ghee in a small sauté pan over medium heat until it has melted. To make the optional garlic butter, add the garlic and cook for 1 to 2 minutes until it is fragrant. Remove the pan from the heat and stir in the parsley or cilantro, if desired. (You can also strain out the garlic chunks if you prefer the garlic butter to be completely smooth.)

Once the dough is ready, transfer it to a floured work surface and shape it into a circle. Cut the dough into six equally sized wedges and roll each wedge into a ball with your hands. Then use a rolling pin to roll out the dough ball until it forms an oval about ¼ inch (6 mm) thick.

At this point the dough can be cooked in the traditional way on a flat pan on the stove, or in the oven.

To cook on the stove, heat a tawa or other flat pan over medium-high heat. Sprinkle some water on one side of the naan dough. Place the wet side down on the pan and cover the pan with a lid. Cook it for 2 minutes, until the dough puffs up. Once the naan starts bubbling and the dough starts drying, flip the naan and cook it for 1 more minute with the lid covering the pan, or until the bread turns golden brown. Once it is cooked, flip the bread again and brush the cooked naan with the melted ghee or the optional garlic butter. Remove it from the pan and cover it with a cloth to keep warm until serving.

To cook the naan in the oven, set the oven to broil. Line a baking tray with foil or parchment paper. Place the ovals of rolled naan on a lined baking tray, put it on the top rack in the oven and broil for 1 to 2 minutes. Flip the naan over and broil for 2 more minutes. Brush the cooked naan with the melted ghee or optional garlic butter.

The cooked naan is best used within 2 or 3 days and should be stored in plastic wrap.

The dough will freeze for up to 1 month and keep in the refrigerator for 1 week.

If the dough is frozen or kept in the freezer, bring it to room temperature before cooking.

Buns, Baguettes and Mini Breads

Brioche? Yes please! These keto brioche buns will definitely make your low-carb lifestyle easier and more delicious! This recipe is especially versatile and is my go-to recipe for perfect high-protein baguettes but can be shaped according to your needs. Whatever the variation you choose, you'll be especially pleased with the golden surface and perfect crumb. Using the optional wheat-flavored extract gives the buns a very traditional taste.

Serves 8   Total carbs: 13 g   Net carbs: 5 g   Fat: 8 g   Protein: 18 g

---

1¼ cups (150 g) vital wheat gluten

½ cup (56 g) oat fiber

¼ cup (37 g) golden flaxseed meal

2 tbsp (16 g) arrowroot flour

1–1½ tsp (10–15 g) kosher salt

2 tbsp (29 g) heavy cream powder

½ tsp xanthan gum or 1 tsp dough conditioner

1 tbsp (20 g) allulose or granulated erythritol

¼ cup (50 g) granulated erythritol (optional, for sweeter bread)

1 tbsp (9 g) instant or active dry yeast

1 cup (240 ml) warm water (100–110°F [38–43°C])

1 tbsp (12 g) honey, sugar or maple syrup (to feed the yeast)

2 tbsp (28 g) unsalted butter or organic keto-friendly shortening

2 eggs, lightly beaten

10 drops wheat-flavored extract (optional)

In a medium bowl, whisk the vital wheat gluten, oat fiber, golden flaxseed meal, arrowroot flour, salt, heavy cream powder, xanthan gum and allulose. Add additional erythritol with the allulose if a sweeter bread is desired. Set the bowl aside.

If you're using active dry yeast, activate the yeast by combining it with the warm water and 1 tablespoon (12 g) of honey, sugar or maple syrup in a 4-quart (4-L) mixing bowl (or stand mixer with the paddle attachment). Give it a quick stir and let this rest until the yeast appears foamy on the surface, about 5 minutes. If you're using rapid rise yeast, no activation is needed. Simply combine the yeast with the warm water and the honey, sugar or maple syrup, give it a quick stir, and move on to the next step.

Add the unsalted butter, beaten eggs and wheat-flavored extract (if using) to the yeast mixture. Whisk this for 30 seconds. Pour the flour mixture into the bowl and mix it until a dough forms. Switch from the paddle attachment to the dough hook and, on medium speed, knead for 7 minutes (or knead with your hands on a lightly floured surface for 10 minutes) until the dough is smooth and stretchy. This is a heavy dough and will require a lot of kneading.

(continued)

Tip: If your kitchen is cold, give your dough some help! Heat the oven to 150°F (66°C). Turn the oven off, place the baking sheet with the dough balls inside and keep the door slightly ajar. This will be a warm environment for your dough to rise. After about 30 minutes, close the oven door to trap the air inside with the rising dough. When it's doubled in size, remove it from the oven.

Buns, Baguettes *and* Mini Breads (cont.)

1 egg, beaten, for egg wash

1 tbsp (15 ml) water

1 tbsp (9 g) sesame seeds, coarse salt, or your choice of sprinkling, for toppings

Put the dough ball back into the mixer bowl and cover the bowl with plastic wrap or a kitchen towel. Let the dough rest at room temperature for 20 minutes.

Line a large baking sheet with parchment paper. Turn the dough out onto a clean surface and divide it into eight pieces. Form each piece into a ball by rolling it on the countertop with a cupped hand. Place each ball onto the baking sheet and cover them with plastic wrap. Let the buns rise for 2 hours, or until noticeably puffy.

Preheat the oven to 375°F (190°C).

Whisk together 1 egg and 1 tablespoon (15 ml) of water to make the egg wash. Brush the egg wash onto each bun, lightly covering all surfaces except the very bottom. Sprinkle on the sesame seeds or other topping of your choice. Bake the buns for 18 to 22 minutes, or until they're dark golden brown. Let the buns cool on a wire rack and serve.

Baking Tip: Egg wash or butter? Egg yolk provides rich color, browning easily in the oven. Water added to an egg wash helps to thin the wash, so it brushes more easily. Melted butter will give the bread a softer crust and richer flavor.

Focaccia *di Zia Lucia*

What could be nicer with soup or salad than fresh focaccia? Of course, this focaccia not only looks, tastes and smells good, but it also fits your keto requirements! The optional sourdough-flavored extract gives this focaccia a very traditional taste. You will be so happy to have this recipe to add that satisfying crunch that only a good bread can give to a meal!

Serves 12   Total carbs: 7 g   Net carbs: 3 g   Fat: 12 g   Protein: 16 g

---

1½ cups (180 g) vital wheat gluten

¼ cup (25 g) oat flour

⅔ cup (60 g) lupin flour

¼ cup (25 g) almond flour

2 tbsp (18 g) kosher salt

1 tbsp (14 g) heavy cream powder

2 tbsp (14 g) wheat protein 5000

1 tsp dough conditioner

1 tbsp (13 g) powdered erythritol

1 tbsp (9 g) instant or active dry yeast

1½ cups (360 ml) warm water (100–110°F [38–43°C]), divided

1 tbsp (12 g) honey, sugar or maple syrup (to feed the yeast)

¼ cup (60 ml) plus 6 tbsp (90 ml) extra virgin olive oil, divided

10 drops sourdough-flavored extract (optional)

In a medium bowl, whisk the vital wheat gluten, oat flour, lupin flour, almond flour, salt, heavy cream powder, wheat protein 5000, dough conditioner and powdered erythritol. Set the bowl aside.

If you're using active dry yeast, combine it with ¾ cup (180 ml) of the warm water and the honey in a large bowl or the bowl of your mixer. Give it a quick stir, then let it rest until the yeast appears foamy on the surface, about 5 minutes. If you're using rapid rise yeast, no activation is needed. Simply combine the yeast with the ¾ cup (180 ml) of warm water and the honey and give it a quick stir before proceeding.

Add the remaining water, ¼ cup (60 ml) of olive oil and sourdough-flavored extract (if using). Beat them together on low speed of an electric mixer with the paddle attachment for 20 seconds, then add the flour mixture. Beat on low speed for 2 minutes, then knead the dough with the dough attachment for 5 minutes. The dough should still feel a little soft, but it should not stick to your hands. Poke it with your finger—if it slowly bounces back, your dough is ready to rise. If not, keep kneading.

Lightly grease a large bowl with 1 tablespoon (15 ml) of olive oil. Place the dough in the bowl, turning it to coat all sides in the oil. Cover the bowl with plastic wrap or a clean kitchen towel. Allow the dough to rise at room temperature for 2 hours.

Generously grease a 9 x 13–inch (23 x 33–cm) baking pan (with at least 1-inch [2.5-cm]-tall sides) with 2 tablespoons (30 ml) of olive oil. This is the base layer of the bread, so be generous with the oil. A pastry brush is helpful to spread it.

(continued)

Focaccia *di Zia Lucia* (cont.)

2 cloves garlic, minced

3–4 tbsp (8–10 g) chopped fresh herbs such as basil, thyme or rosemary (or 2 tbsp [4 g] dried herbs)

Sprinkle of coarse salt and freshly ground black pepper

Tip: If your kitchen is cold, give the dough a slightly warmer place to rise. Heat the oven to 150°F (66°C). Turn the oven off, place the dough inside and keep the door slightly ajar. This will be a warm environment for rising. After about 30 minutes, close the oven door to trap the air inside with the rising dough. When it's doubled in size, remove it from the oven.

When the dough is ready, punch it down to release any air bubbles. Place the dough on the oiled baking pan, then stretch and flatten the dough to fit the pan. Don't tear the dough. If it's shrinking, cover it with a clean towel and let it rest for 5 to 10 minutes before continuing.

Cover the dough tightly and let it rest in the refrigerator for at least 1 hour and up to 24 hours. The longer it rests, the better the flavor. I recommend at least 12 hours.

Remove the dough from the refrigerator and let it sit at room temperature as you preheat the oven and prepare the toppings. Keep it covered. It may rise a little during this time, but not much.

Preheat the oven to 400°F (200°C). Allow the oven to heat for at least 10 to 15 minutes so every inch of the oven is very hot. Whisk the remaining 3 tablespoons (45 ml) of olive oil with the minced garlic and herbs, then, using your fingers, dimple the dough all over the surface. Drizzle on the olive oil topping and use your hands or a pastry brush to spread it all over the top. Add a little more olive oil if needed so the dough is completely covered. Sprinkle the dough with a little coarse salt and freshly ground black pepper.

Bake for 25 to 30 minutes, or until lightly browned on top. If desired, broil on high for the last minute to really brown the top.

Cut the focaccia and serve it hot or let it come to room temperature before slicing and serving. Focaccia tastes wonderful warm or at room temperature. Cover any leftover focaccia tightly and store it at room temperature for 2 days or in the refrigerator for 1 week. You can also freeze the baked and cooled focaccia for up to 3 months, thawing it in the refrigerator or at room temperature. To reheat the slices, you can use the microwave or bake them in a 300°F (149°C) oven for 5 minutes.

Leili's **Perfect Pastry Dough**

This pastry is buttery, flaky and layered as it should be—and you'll be glad to know that the yeast consumes the sugar used in proofing, so no extra carbs are added! This recipe is my pride and joy because I have tested it so extensively and found it to be perfect for both savory and sweet fillings (note that the savory dough uses less sweetener and adds herbes de Provence). Be sure to spoon and level the flours as you measure!

You'll use this pastry dough as a unique element of a number of recipes in this book, including Savory Mushroom Galette (page 50), Keto Beef Wellington (page 12) and individual pastries.

Makes 2 (12 x 8-inch [30 x 20-cm]) sheets
Serves 20   Total carbs: 5 g   Net carbs: 1 g   Fat: 8 g   Protein: 5 g

---

½ cup (65 g) vital wheat gluten

⅔ cup (60 g) oat fiber, plus more for generously flouring hands, surface and dough

⅔ cup (65 g) lupin flour

2 tbsp (8 g) wheat protein 5000 (or whey protein)

1 tsp salt

1 tbsp (14 g) heavy cream powder

½ tsp xanthan gum powder

1 tsp herbes de Provence (for savory dough only)

½ cup (116 ml) warm water (100–110°F [38–43°C])

2¼ tsp (7 g) active dry or instant yeast

1 tbsp (12 g) honey, sugar or maple syrup (to feed the yeast)

1 tbsp (14 g) granulated erythritol for savory dough or ¼ cup (25 g) granulated erythritol for sweet dough

¼ cup (60 ml) whole milk or any nondairy milk, at room temperature (68–72°F [20–22°C])

1 large egg, at room temperature

12 tbsp (170 g) unsalted butter, cold

In a medium bowl, whisk the vital wheat gluten, oat fiber, lupin flour, wheat protein, salt, heavy cream powder, xanthan gum powder and herbes de Provence (if making savory dough). Set the bowl aside.

Whisk the warm water, yeast, and honey together in a large bowl. Cover and allow to rest until foamy on top, about 5 minutes. Whisk in the granulated erythritol—1 tablespoon (14 g) for savory dough or ¼ cup (25 g) for sweet dough—the milk and egg. Once these wet ingredients are mixed together, lightly cover and set the bowl aside.

Cut the cold butter into ¼-inch (6-mm) slices and add it to a food processor or blender, then add the flour mixture on top. Pulse gently to mix the cold butter into the flour, working quickly so that the butter remains cold. (If you don't have a food processor, you can use a pastry cutter to work in the butter.)

(continued)

Leili's **Perfect Pastry Dough (cont.)**

Pour the flour mixture into the wet yeast mixture in the large bowl. Very gently fold everything together using a rubber spatula or wooden spoon. Treat the mixture gently, like pie dough, folding *just until* the dry ingredients are moistened. The butter must remain in pieces and crumbles, which creates a flaky pastry. Turn the sticky dough out onto a large piece of plastic wrap, cover it up tightly and refrigerate it for at least 4 hours and up to 48 hours.

Take the dough out of the refrigerator to begin the "rolling and folding" process. Very generously flour a work surface, your hands and a rolling pin with oat fiber. The dough is very sticky, so make sure you have more flour nearby as you roll and fold. Using the palm of your hands, gently flatten the dough into a small square. Using a rolling pin, roll the dough out into a 15 x 8–inch (38 x 20–cm) rectangle. When needed, flour the work surface and dough as you are rolling. Fold the dough into thirds as if it were a business letter. Turn it clockwise and roll it out into a 15-inch (38-cm)-long rectangle again. Then fold it into thirds again. Turn it clockwise. You'll repeat rolling and folding one more time for a total of three times.

Wrap the folded dough with plastic wrap and seal it tightly. Refrigerate the dough for at least 1 hour and up to 24 hours. You can also freeze the dough at this point. (See the freezing instructions below.)

Take the dough out of the refrigerator and cut it in half. It is easier to work with half the recipe at a time. If you want to bake it right away, roll out one 12 x 8–inch (30 x 20–cm) sheet, wrapping the remaining sheet for later use if desired.

This pastry dough can be refrigerated for up to 48 hours. During or after the second chilling time, you could also freeze the dough for up to 1 month. For freezing, I prefer to wrap the dough in plastic and then place that in a plastic bag or container for further storage. (I don't recommend freezing the dough before the rolling and folding step.) Thaw the dough overnight in the refrigerator, then use it for your desired recipe.

Small Temptations

Sometimes it's the little things, like crunchy snacks or gooey cheese, that are the joys of eating. Those joys aren't too far away with these family favorite recipes! They're the ones that you'll pack in lunches and serve on Saturday nights because the kids ask for them. You'll be glad they are on the "yummy" list because you'll look forward to enjoying them too! You'll be happy to find some new, surprising keto favorites like Daisy's Hush Puppies (page 85) and Cheesy, Crunchy Mozzarella Sticks (page 81) in this chapter.

Have fun with these classic snacks and international favorites. This keto food is far from boring, and you'll be proud to share these at your table.

Upper Crust Chicken Nuggets

Crispy chicken nuggets are a great party food, afternoon snack or a small meal for children who love to pick up the little bite-sized patties. The crust is the secret to these tasty morsels: keto-friendly crushed pork rinds with a zing of hot sauce star here to make everyone come back for seconds. They'll never suspect this is a keto recipe!

Serves 6   Total carbs: 1 g   Net carbs: 1 g   Fat: 18 g   Protein: 44 g

---

2 boneless, skinless chicken breasts, cut into cubes (about 1½ lb [680 g] total)

1½ tsp (8 g) plus ½ tsp kosher salt, plus more to taste, divided

¼ tsp onion powder

¼ tsp pepper

1 tbsp (14 g) salted butter, melted

1 cup (32 g) crumbled pork rinds

½ cup (45 g) grated Parmesan cheese

1 tsp smoked paprika

½ tsp dried parsley

¼ tsp garlic powder

3 eggs, beaten

Hot sauce (optional)

1½–2 cups (375–470 ml) avocado oil, for frying

Place the cubed chicken in the bowl of a food processor. Add in 1½ teaspoons (8 g) of salt, the onion powder, pepper and butter. Process until it resembles a fine paste.

With wet hands, roll and flatten the chicken mixture into 30 small nugget patties, using about 1 tablespoon (28 g) of the meat mixture for each nugget.

For the breading, place the crumbled pork rinds, Parmesan cheese, ½ teaspoon of salt, paprika, dried parsley and garlic powder onto a large plate and mix them to combine. Pour the eggs into a small bowl and mix them with hot sauce to taste, as desired. Roll the chicken nuggets in the pork rind mixture, then the egg mixture and then back in the pork rind mixture. Transfer the breaded nuggets to a baking sheet in preparation for frying.

If you're frying the nuggets, heat the oil in a cast-iron skillet or heavy-bottomed pot over medium heat. If you're baking the nuggets, preheat the oven to 375°F (190°C).

If frying, fry the nuggets in the avocado oil, in batches, for 4 to 5 minutes total, or until they are golden brown and cooked through (165°F [74°C]). Transfer the nuggets to a paper towel–lined plate to drain and season them generously with salt while they are still warm.

If baking, transfer the nuggets to a parchment-lined baking sheet and bake them for 15 minutes on the middle rack, just until cooked through, flipping them over halfway through baking. Remove them from the oven and let the nuggets rest a few minutes before serving. Don't overbake your nuggets or they will start to get dry.

Serve the nuggets immediately with a side of your favorite sauce like sugar-free ketchup.

Bacon, Bacon, Bacon *and* Cheddar Mashed Potatoes

American comfort food often includes mashed potatoes and cheese. And anything is better with bacon, right? Try this easy dinner fare when everyone comes home tired and cranky from hunger. After they have devoured it, they'll ask for more mashed potatoes (but this is really cauliflower). Plan ahead to accommodate extra helpings because this is a favorite!

Serves 4   Total carbs: 9 g   Net carbs: 5 g   Fat: 31 g   Protein: 15 g

1 lb (454 g) cauliflower

1 tbsp (15 ml) white vinegar

3 tbsp (42 g) salted butter

¼ tsp garlic powder

¼ cup (23 g) grated Parmesan cheese

½ tsp onion powder

¼ cup (60 ml) sour cream

4 oz (112 g) cream cheese

2 tbsp (30 g) heavy whipping cream powder (optional)

2 tbsp (6 g) snipped chives, divided

1 cup (90 g) grated Cheddar cheese

4 slices bacon, cooked and crumbled, divided

Salt and pepper, to taste

Cut out the stem and core from the cauliflower and dice it into small pieces. Cook it in a large pot of boiling salted water and the white vinegar until the cauliflower is tender but not too soft. Drain it well and mash it with a potato masher or electric hand mixer. Leave some chunks for texture.

Mix the mashed cauliflower in a large bowl with the butter, garlic powder, Parmesan cheese, onion powder, sour cream, cream cheese and heavy whipping cream powder (if using) until it resembles the consistency of mashed potatoes. Add most of the chives, saving some to add to the top later. Add the Cheddar cheese and most of the crumbled cooked bacon and mix by hand. Season it with salt and pepper.

Top it with the remaining crumbled cooked bacon and chives.

Tip: If at any point the cheese isn't melting into the mashed cauliflower, you can set the stove's heat to the lowest heat setting and place the dish on top. This will warm it just enough so that everything combines.

Perfectly Golden **French Fries**

These French fries are inspired by a delicious Indian snack called suji fries. Traditionally made from semolina flour, they have a flavor that was a challenge to replicate from my keto toolbox, but wait until you taste these! The fries taste like a really good French fry, with a satisfying crunchy texture—just what you've been missing on your keto journey. My boys ask for these fries often, and of course they don't have any idea that they are getting lots of protein and low carbs—they just like to eat them.

Serves 2   **Total carbs: 16 g**   **Net carbs: 5 g**   **Fat: 51 g**   **Protein: 20 g**

¼ cup (35 g) sesame seeds

¼ cup (32 g) nutritional yeast powder

¼ cup (27 g) golden flaxseed meal

2 tbsp (16 g) coconut flour or ¼ cup (25 g) almond flour

2 tsp (5 g) xanthan gum powder

10 drops mashed potato flavor (optional)

⅓ cup (79 ml) water

½ tsp salt, plus more to taste

1 cup (235 ml) avocado oil

Olive oil spray, for air frying

Add the sesame seeds, nutritional yeast powder and golden flaxseed meal to a food processor and pulse until evenly combined. Add the coconut flour, xanthan gum powder and mashed potato flavor (if using) and mix well. Set this aside.

Heat the water in a small pan until it boils, then add the salt and remove it from the heat. Add the flour mixture to the water and stir it for 1 minute. Transfer the dough onto a piece of parchment paper and knead it for 2 minutes.

Place another piece of parchment paper on top and roll the dough with a rolling pin to about ½-inch (1.3-cm) thickness, then cut the dough into ½-inch (1.3-cm)-wide fingers like French fries.

To a large skillet, add enough avocado oil to cover the keto French fries as they cook. Heat the oil over medium heat. Once the oil is heated, add a single layer of fries to the oil and let them cook until they are golden brown on all sides, about 1 minute. You may need to turn them to cook all sides. Remove them from the oil and onto a paper towel–lined plate. Sprinkle them with additional salt if needed.

To air fry, spread the French fries onto the air fryer basket or tray in a single layer. Spray the fries with olive oil. Air fry them at 400°F (200°C) for 6 minutes.

Cheesy, Crunchy Mozzarella Sticks

My family thought that our keto journey would mean the end of yummy snacks like fried mozzarella sticks. Ha! I've just found a better way to make them. Each stick has less than 1 gram of net carbs, but that does not seem to matter to the guys in my house—they are gone soon after I make them! We love to dip them into low-carb marinara sauce.

Serves 3   Total carbs: 6 g   Net carbs: 3 g   Fat: 18 g   Protein: 27 g

---

6 mozzarella string cheese sticks, frozen

$\frac{1}{2}$ cup (50 g) almond flour

1 large egg

$\frac{1}{8}$ tsp salt, plus more to taste

$\frac{1}{8}$ tsp freshly ground black pepper

$\frac{1}{4}$ cup (24 g) unflavored whey protein

1 tbsp (3 g) Italian seasoning

1 tsp smoked paprika

$\frac{1}{3}$ cup (30 g) grated Parmesan cheese

$\frac{1}{2}$ tsp garlic powder

$\frac{1}{4}$ tsp onion powder

Oil, for deep frying

Cut the individual cheese sticks in half so that there will be 12 sticks, each $\frac{1}{2}$ inch (1.3 cm) wide and 2 inches (5 cm) long.

To toast the almond flour in a skillet, simply add the flour to a nonstick skillet over medium heat for 1 minute, stirring occasionally to prevent scorching. This isn't required, but it helps with the coating texture!

Place the egg in a bowl with the salt and black pepper and whisk to combine. Mix the toasted flour, whey protein, Italian seasoning, smoked paprika, grated Parmesan cheese, garlic powder, onion powder and salt to taste in a shallow dish.

Take each frozen cheese stick and dip it into the egg, letting the excess drip off. Then coat each cheese stick in the breading mixture, shaking off the excess, and place it on a plate.

Once each cheese stick has been breaded, take each one through the egg and breading again for a second coating, paying attention to cover the ends completely, and return the sticks to the freezer for 10 more minutes to make them easier to handle. Place the mozzarella sticks in an airtight container and freeze them for 2 hours.

Preheat the oven to 400°F (200°C). Bake the frozen mozzarella sticks for 8 to 10 minutes, flipping once halfway through. Serve them hot with your favorite sauce if desired. Enjoy!

To air fry, place the coated mozzarella sticks in the air fryer in a single layer. Cook at 375°F (190°C) for 10 to 12 minutes depending on your air fryer.

To deep fry, completely freeze the coated cheese sticks. Bring the oil in the fryer to 365°F (185°C). Carefully lower the mozzarella sticks into the hot oil, a few at a time, and cook them for approximately 1 minute. Remove them from the oil and drain them on paper towels.

Crispy Coconut Shrimp Croccante

Is this a crowd-pleaser? You bet. Shrimp sautéed with a crispy almond flour and coconut coating are magic, and the sweet chili dipping sauce made with allulose is just the right accompaniment. No one will suspect that this crunchy recipe is from your keto collection—they'll just enjoy these tasty shrimp!

Serves 6   Total carbs: 6 g   Net carbs: 2 g   Fat: 21 g   Protein: 26 g

Shrimp

1 lb (454 g) raw large shrimp, peeled and deveined, with tails

½ cup (50 g) superfine almond flour

½ tsp salt

½ tsp ground black pepper

½ tsp onion powder

½ tsp garlic powder

2 large eggs, beaten

¾ cup (75 g) unflavored protein powder

1 cup (100 g) unsweetened shredded coconut

Avocado oil or coconut oil for frying (I prefer frying the coconut shrimp in coconut oil for the best taste)

Cooking spray, for baking

Sweet Chili Dipping Sauce

¼ tsp xanthan gum

5 tbsp (63 g) granulated allulose sweetener

4 tbsp (60 ml) hot sauce

3 cloves garlic, chopped

2 tsp (4 g) ginger, chopped

2 tbsp (30 ml) lime juice, fresh

¼ cup (60 ml) water

1 tsp lime zest

Parsley, for garnish (optional)

To prepare the shrimp, rinse them in cold water and pat them dry with paper towels.

Set up three medium shallow bowls. Combine the almond flour, salt, pepper, onion powder and garlic powder in one bowl. Beat the eggs in the second bowl. Combine the protein powder and unsweetened shredded coconut in the third bowl.

Next, one by one, dip the shrimp into each mixture while holding onto the shrimp's tail. Make sure that each shrimp is evenly coated by each mixture. Start by dipping the shrimp in the almond flour mixture. Next, dip the shrimp in the egg mixture. Finally, dip the shrimp in the coconut mixture, flipping as necessary to coat each side.

If frying, place a large pan over medium heat and add enough oil to generously cover the bottom, about ¼ inch (6 mm) deep. Once the oil is hot (350°F [177°C]), add the shrimp and sauté for 2 minutes per side, or until golden brown and the shrimp is pink and cooked through. Cook the shrimp in batches and don't overcrowd the pan. When thoroughly cooked, transfer the shrimp to a plate lined with paper towels to soak up the excess oil.

To bake the shrimp in a regular oven, generously spray both sides of the shrimp with cooking spray and bake at 400°F (200°C) for 15 to 20 minutes, flipping the shrimp halfway through.

To make the sauce, in a small saucepan, whisk together the xanthan gum and the granulated allulose until combined.

Next, turn the heat on medium low and whisk in the hot sauce, garlic and ginger. Then gradually add the lime juice and water while whisking. Bring the sauce barely to a simmer and then remove it from the heat and stir in the lime zest.

Serve the shrimp with the dipping sauce and garnish with fresh parsley, if desired.

Daisy's Hush Puppies

Hush, puppy! That's what Daisy, our country friend, might say as she throws a bit of fried breading to a barking dog. Actually, hush puppies are a popular side dish for fried fish in the southern United States. Corn meal is used to batter the fish and also to make crispy fried dough balls. They've become so popular that many people just eat hush puppies as appetizers or snacks, and children ask for them! Whole fat buttermilk is a secret ingredient in this recipe, but if you cannot find it, add 1½ tablespoons (22 ml) of vinegar to ½ cup (120 ml) of half-and-half and let it sit undisturbed for 10 minutes and you'll have a tasty substitution.

Serves 6   Total carbs: 6 g   Net carbs: 3 g   Fat: 17 g   Protein: 8 g

1 cup (100 g) finely ground almond flour

1 cup (100 g) fine sunflower flour

2 tbsp (14 g) flaxseed meal

1 tsp baking powder

1 tsp salt

1 tsp onion powder

¼ tsp cayenne pepper

3 tbsp (18 g) chopped scallions

2 tbsp (30 ml) whole fat buttermilk

¼ cup (60 ml) heavy whipping cream

1 egg, beaten

High-quality oil, for frying

Salted butter, for serving

In a medium bowl, stir together the almond flour, sunflower flour, flaxseed meal, baking powder, salt, onion powder and cayenne pepper. Stir in the scallions, buttermilk, heavy whipping cream and beaten egg, mixing until blended. Do not overmix.

Chill the dough in the refrigerator for 1 hour to make it easier to handle.

Preheat 2 inches (5 cm) of oil (avocado oil, or any oil with a high smoke point) in a deep fryer or large heavy pot to 365°F (185°C). Using a thermometer will help keep the oil at a constant temperature.

Form 12 hush puppies from the chilled dough using two spoons to shape them and gently drop them into the oil. Let the hush puppies cook until they are golden brown, 2 to 3 minutes. Transfer them with a slotted spoon to a sheet pan lined with paper towels to drain. Repeat with the remaining batter, adjusting the heat to maintain the oil temperature. Serve them hot with salted butter. Yum!

Hush puppies can also be cooked in the air fryer. Set the air fryer to 400°F (200°C). Place the formed dough into the basket of the air fryer, being careful that the hush puppies are not touching one another. Air fry for 4 minutes, shake or flip the hush puppies, and then air fry them until they are done, 4 to 5 more minutes.

You'll love popping these hush puppies into your mouth as soon as they are cooked, but if there are any left, they'll keep for a day at room temperature.

 Breadsticks

Keto breadsticks? You bet! My Perfect Pastry Dough (page 68) makes an
excellent base for these crunchy snacks. A bit of pesto and a coating of
Parmesan cheese give these breadsticks great Italian flavor.
Watch them disappear!

Serves 10 **Total carbs: 6 g** **Net carbs: 2 g** **Fat: 16 g** **Protein: 10 g**

---

1 sheet Leili's Perfect Pastry
Dough (page 68)

½ cup (125 g) pesto

½ cup (45 g) grated Parmesan
cheese

1 egg, beaten, for brushing the
top

1 tbsp (9 g) sesame seeds

2 tbsp (28 g) salted butter,
melted

Preheat the oven to 400°F (200°C). Line a baking sheet with parchment
paper.

Place the pastry dough on parchment paper that is the size of a rectangular
baking sheet. Use a rolling pin and make a rectangle, about ¼ inch
(6 mm) thick.

Spread the pesto over the dough and sprinkle it evenly with the Parmesan
cheese. Press lightly on the cheese to help it stick to the dough and
pesto layers.

Using a pizza cutter or sharp knife, cut the dough into 1-inch (2.5-cm) strips.

Fold the strips in half lengthwise and twist them together. Place the twisted
strips on the parchment-lined baking sheet about 1 inch (2.5 cm) apart.
Brush the twists with the beaten egg and sprinkle the sesame seeds on top.

Bake the breadsticks for 15 to 17 minutes, or until golden brown. Brush
them with melted butter and serve immediately.

Store leftovers in an airtight container in the refrigerator for 5 days.

Mini **Tuna Sandwich**

Here's a recipe where my Lovin' Loaf (Bread) (page 56) really shines. You'll appreciate the perfect taste and texture of the bread that complements a flavorful tuna salad. The extra veggies give the salad more body and extra crunch, making a very satisfying lunch. You'll be so glad you have this surprising bread in your keto toolbox!

Serves 3   Total carbs: 13   Net carbs: 5 g   Fat: 25 g   Protein: 23 g

---

1 (5-oz [140-g]) can tuna, preferably packed in olive oil, drained

½ ripe (100 g) avocado, chopped

½ cup (50 g) minced celery

¼ cup (13 g) minced red onion

2 tbsp (30 ml) sour cream

2 tbsp (30 g) cream cheese, softened

2 tsp (10 ml) lemon juice

Salt and pepper, to taste

1 tsp lemon zest

2 tbsp (6 g) fresh dill or parsley, chopped

Olive oil, as needed

1 tbsp (15 g) mayonnaise

6 toasted slices Lovin' Loaf (Bread) (page 56)

In a medium bowl, add the tuna and use a fork to gently separate the pieces. Add the chopped avocado, minced celery and minced red onion. Mix with a fork, then add the sour cream, cream cheese and lemon juice. Sprinkle a little salt and pepper to taste and add the lemon zest and chopped fresh dill. Chill the tuna mixture in the refrigerator for 30 minutes.

Add olive oil or salt and pepper, if necessary. Spread the mayonnaise on each slice of bread. Spread 3 slices with the tuna mixture. Top each with the remaining bread slices. Cut each sandwich into four triangles for mini sandwiches. Tuna salad will keep in an airtight container in the fridge for up to 5 days.

Rosemary Grissini

Do you miss a crunchy breadstick with your meal? That extra bit of flavor and snap can make a nice entrée or snack more satisfying, and these keto-friendly grissini make it easy to share. Rosemary or sesame are classic flavors for grissini; try poppy seed, thyme or coarse salt and pepper for variety. The optional rye flavor gives some extra depth to the other flavors. My rosemary grissini have been known to disappear from the table quickly, so be sure you get some or plan for a double batch!

Serves 12   Total carbs: 5 g   Net carbs: 2 g   Fat: 11 g   Protein: 8 g

---

1½ cups (150 g) almond flour

½ cup (50 g) sesame seed flour

¼ cup (25 g) lupin flour

1 tsp garlic powder

1 tsp baking powder

½ tsp xanthan gum

½ tsp salt

2 large eggs

3 tbsp (45 ml) almond milk

1 tsp olive oil

2 tsp (6 g) chopped fresh rosemary leaves

10 drops rye flavor (optional)

1 large egg yolk, for brushing

1 tsp sea salt or pink Himalayan salt flakes

4 tbsp (35 g) sesame seeds, poppy seeds or grated Parmesan cheese

Preheat the oven to 375°F (190°C) and move the oven rack to slightly below the middle position. Line a baking tray with parchment paper.

Sift the almond flour, sesame seed flour, lupin flour, garlic powder, baking powder, xanthan gum and salt together over a large mixing bowl and stir to combine. Add the eggs, almond milk, olive oil, chopped rosemary and rye flavor (if using). Mix well until a ball of dough forms.

Divide the dough into equal pieces, each weighing about 25 grams. Roll each piece into a log that is roughly 12 x ½ inches (30 x 1.3 cm).

Place the rolled out dough onto the prepared baking tray, allowing sufficient space between the sticks. Brush them with the egg yolk and sprinkle them with the sea salt and sesame seeds.

Bake the grissini for 15 minutes, then lower the heat to 350°F (177°C) and bake them for an additional 15 minutes.

The grissini must be completely cool before storing in an airtight container for 2 weeks.

Stuffed Grape Leaves (*Dolmeh*)

One of my early memories of a holiday celebration in my Persian family was the huge platter with a carefully constructed tower of *dolmeh*, or stuffed grape leaves. It was right at my eye level on the table, and I found it most intriguing. When it was time to eat, I felt like I had discovered something new: a perfect little cylinder of rice and herbs. Of course, most Balkan and Middle Eastern celebrations feature versions of this dish, but for me, dolmeh are special. Your keto lifestyle can welcome dolmeh too with my meat-based recipe accented with just the right flavorful sugar-free sauce. These dolmeh taste very much like my precious memories. Be sure to make lots to share!

Serves 6   Total carbs: 12 g   Net carbs: 4 g   Fat: 14 g   Protein: 14 g

Dolmeh

2 tbsp (30 ml) olive oil, divided

1 large onion, finely chopped

2 cloves garlic, minced

½ lb (227 g) ground beef

1 cup (112 g) riced cauliflower

½ tsp salt

½ tsp black pepper

¼ cup (24 g) fresh tarragon, chopped, or 2 tsp (2 g) dried tarragon

¼ cup (15 g) fresh parsley, chopped, or 2 tsp (2 g) dried parsley

¼ cup (8 g) fresh cilantro, chopped, or 2 tsp (2 g) dried cilantro

¼ cup (8 g) fresh dill, chopped, or 2 tsp (2 g) dried dill

2 tbsp (20 g) hemp hearts

¼ tsp turmeric

1 tbsp (9 g) walnuts, ground

1 (16-oz [454-g]) jar grape leaves, drained

1 cup (235 ml) chicken broth or bone broth

To make the dolmeh, heat 1 tablespoon (15 ml) of olive oil in a pan over medium heat. Sauté the onion and garlic until golden brown, 2 or 3 minutes. Add in the ground beef and brown it, about 10 minutes. Add the riced cauliflower to the browned ground beef. Add the salt and pepper. Stir in the chopped tarragon, parsley, cilantro, dill, hemp hearts and turmeric and cook for a few minutes. Finally, add the walnuts and cook for a few minutes, stirring occasionally. Set the mixture aside to cool.

To wrap the dolmeh, rinse and dry the grape leaves to remove any excess salt. Reserve three grape leaves to line the pot.

Lay a grape leaf flat on your working surface, rough side up. If the grape leaf has deep edges, place another grape leaf on top so you have a bigger surface to work with. Trim off the little stems to make them easier to roll.

Spoon 1 tablespoon (25 g) of the filling in the top of the leaf. Roll up the leaf halfway to the top edge. Carefully fold the edges from the sides and overlap them to cover the filling. Continue to wrap the dolmeh into a cylinder. Repeat, filling all the leaves.

To layer the dolmeh in the pot, pour 1 tablespoon (15 ml) of olive oil into the pot and cover the bottom with three grape leaves.

Place the stuffed grape leaves tightly next to each other, overlapping side down. Repeat this step until the bottom of the pot is covered. Make sure the stuffed grape leaves are tightly set next to each other so that they won't open up while cooking. Repeat the layers until every dolmeh is in the pot.

(continued)

Syrup

1½ cups (352 ml) hot water

¼ cup (50 g) brown sugar substitute

¼ cup (60 ml) wine vinegar

¼ cup (60 ml) fresh lemon juice

1 tbsp (10 g) dried barberries or unsweetened cranberries, for garnish (optional)

Pour the chicken broth into the pot, then place a heatproof plate or a saucepan lid directly on top of the stuffed grape leaves and press a bit. This step keeps the dolmeh in place in the pot during cooking. Cover the pot with its lid and cook on medium heat. When the broth starts simmering, lower the heat and let the dolmeh cook for about 45 minutes.

Meanwhile, to prepare the syrup, mix the water, brown sugar substitute, wine vinegar and lemon juice in a small bowl.

After 45 minutes, uncover the pot and baste the dolmeh with the syrup. Cover the pot again and let it cook for 15 more minutes, or until the leaves are tender. Taste the sauce and adjust the seasoning. The water must be all absorbed and the grape leaves should be cooked.

Serve garnished with the barberries or cranberries, if using.

Vegetable Samosas *with* Green Chutney

Do you need a make-ahead dinner for busy nights? Crispy vegetable samosas using my Versatile Naan (page 59) dough are perfect! The dough, fragrant filling and spicy cilantro mint chutney can be made in advance, then assembled and fried. I like to make extra cooked filling to keep in the freezer for the next batch. Versatile Naan comes to the rescue for yet another great keto meal!

Serves 6   Total carbs: 16 g   Net carbs: 8 g   Fat: 20 g   Protein: 24 g

---

Filling

2 cups (225 g) riced cauliflower

$1/2$ jicama, chopped (1 cup [130 g])

1 tbsp (15 ml) oil or ghee, plus more to wrap the samosas

$1/2$ tsp cumin seeds

1 medium onion, chopped

$1\frac{1}{2}$ tsp (2 g) jalapeño, minced

1 tsp ground coriander

$1/2$ tsp garam masala

$1/2$ tsp ground turmeric

1 tsp salt

$1/4$ cup (36 g) frozen green peas, thawed

1 batch Versatile Naan dough (page 59)

2 cups (470 ml) oil, for frying

To make the filling, set a medium pot filled with water over medium-high heat. Add the cauliflower and jicama and bring the water to a boil. Boil them until they are fork tender, about 10 minutes.

Set a large skillet over medium-high heat and add the oil. Once the oil shimmers, add the cumin seeds to the skillet. Once they sputter, turn the heat down to medium and add the onion. Sauté the onion for 3 to 4 minutes, or until the onion softens. Add the jalapeño, coriander, garam masala, ground turmeric and salt. Give everything a quick stir. Add the peas.

Drain the cauliflower and jicama and add them to the skillet. Using the back of a wooden spoon or a potato masher, coarsely mash the mixture, leaving no large chunks. Stir to combine. You want it mixed well. In the end, the filling should be relatively dry and thick.

Set the filling aside to cool completely before filling the samosas.

Divide the prepared naan dough into six equal parts. Roll each part into a smooth ball and cover them with a damp cloth. Pick up one ball, press it between your palms to flatten it and lightly dab the surface of the dough with oil or ghee. This prevents the rolling pin from sticking to the dough. Resist the urge to dust the countertop with flour as the loose flour will burn when you drop the dough in the oil to fry, giving the samosa an off taste.

Use a rolling pin to flatten the dough into a circle 6 inches (15 cm) in diameter, 1 millimeter thick. Cut each in half so you have two half-moon shapes from each circle.

If you're having a difficult time rolling out the dough, place the round between pieces of wax paper or parchment.

(continued)

Vegetable Samosas *with* Green Chutney (cont.)

Cilantro Mint Chutney

2 cups (30 g) fresh cilantro, coarsely chopped

1 cup (30 g) fresh mint, coarsely chopped

¼ cup (60 ml) lemon juice, from about 1 large lemon

4–5 cloves garlic

1 jalapeño, chopped

1-inch (2.5-cm) piece ginger root, peeled and chopped

1½ tsp (9 g) salt

1½ tsp (5 g) cumin seeds

To fill the samosa, pick up one half-moon of dough and wet the edges with water using your finger. Line up the edges to make a cone shape. Gently pinch along the edges of the cone, making sure they are sealed.

Add 1½ tablespoons (8 g) of filling to the cone. This should fill it three-quarters of the way. Brush water on the edges of the cone's opening and pinch the edges together to close the samosa.

Repeat with the rest of the dough. Cover the sealed samosas with a damp cloth. In the end, you should have twelve samosas.

To fry the samosas, in a deep pot, add the oil and heat it to 200°F (93°C) over medium heat. Add the samosas to the oil and fry them in batches; do not overcrowd the pot. Fry until the samosas begin to turn golden.

Once the samosas are golden, increase the heat to medium high, bringing the temperature up to 350°F (177°C) and cook them for another 5 minutes until the samosas have darkened to a deeper brown.

Take the samosas out of the oil and transfer them to a plate lined with paper towels.

Before going forward with the next batch of samosas, reduce the heat back to medium or medium low, until the oil temperature drops back to 200°F (93°C). Getting this part right for a samosa is the trickiest part. If you start with high-temperature oil, the pastry will turn soggy and oily. So starting with warm oil and then increasing the heat is the way to go here.

To make the chutney, combine the cilantro, mint, lemon juice, garlic, jalapeño, ginger root, salt and cumin seeds in a blender or food processor. The consistency should be thick enough to coat a samosa when dipped. If you want it thinner, add 2 to 3 tablespoons (30 to 45 ml) of water. Transfer the chutney to a bowl, cover it and wait until the samosas are ready.

Breakfasts to
Brighten Your Day

Where's the fun in starting your day when you're ignoring what you really want to eat? These keto-balanced breakfasts satisfy cravings and keep everyone's carbs in check. Tasty, comforting foods can fit into your keto plan with a few tricks that you will learn to round out your food choices. You'll enjoy them so much that you'll want to share them with guests—and they won't believe these are keto!

Having a hard time convincing your kids to eat well in the morning? You'll find some good choices to tempt them, like the Layered Berry Chia Pudding (page 117), as well as ones they will want to make themselves, like Button Pancakes in a Bowl (page 109) or Waffle Brownies (page 100). Have fun with these recipes that will banish breakfast boredom!

Waffle Brownies

And the winner for best breakfast is . . . waffle brownies! Packed with protein, flavor and extra chocolate chips, these are both delicious and satisfying. There is no guilt with this keto-friendly recipe! Enjoy these on a weekend morning and save some for a weekday treat.

Serves 6   Total carbs: 9 g   Net carbs: 2 g   Fat: 20 g   Protein: 24 g

---

Coconut oil spray or avocado oil spray, to grease the waffle iron

1¼ cups (120 g) almond flour

⅓ cup (35 g) cocoa powder

½ cup (100 g) creamy vanilla-flavored or plain whey protein or egg white protein powder

1 tsp sea salt

1 tsp baking powder

½ cup (100 g) granulated erythritol

¼ cup (56 g) virgin coconut oil, melted (or [56 g] unsalted butter, melted)

4 large eggs

¼ tsp sugar-free vanilla extract

½ cup (120 ml) unsweetened almond milk or cashew milk

¼ cup (60 ml) heavy whipping cream

¼ cup (40 g) sugar-free chocolate chips

Powdered sweetener, berries and/or chocolate syrup, for toppings (optional)

Preheat the waffle iron and spray it with the oil of your choice.

In a medium bowl, using a whisk, combine the almond flour, cocoa powder, whey protein, sea salt, baking powder and granulated erythritol until the mixture is free of lumps

Add the melted coconut oil to the dry ingredients and whisk until it's incorporated. Add the eggs, vanilla, almond milk and heavy whipping cream and stir the batter until it's smooth. Add the chocolate chips. Pour the batter into the waffle maker, close it and cook for a minute or two. (The timing depends on the waffle maker.) Be careful not to overfill, as the batter expands and may overflow the waffle iron.

Dust the waffles with powdered sweetener and top with berries and/or chocolate syrup. Serve immediately. To serve later, cool the waffles, wrap them so they are airtight and refrigerate for 5 days.

Crazy **Glazed Donuts**

Donuts, donuts, donuts! Did you think they were gone from your life forever?

One of my family's traditions for road trips to the country were the fresh donuts that my older sister baked for our picnic lunches. Our favorites were the glazed donuts, and I was the child who was always ready to help by dipping them in the glaze and decorating them. My boys now look forward to finding the craziest pattern in the glaze and ask for the "crazy donuts." Some clever substitutions can make these yummy keto donuts part of your family's memories too. I usually fry them, but you can bake them using the optional baking instructions.

Serves 12   Total carbs: 7 g   Net carbs: 3 g   Fat: 22 g   Protein: 8 g

---

Donuts

2 cups (200 g) almond flour

¼ cup (25 g) creamy vanilla protein powder (or unflavored protein powder)

2½ tsp (12 g) baking powder

½ tsp xanthan gum powder

2 tbsp (12 g) heavy cream powder (optional)

¾ tsp salt

¼ tsp ground nutmeg (or increase to ½ tsp for slightly stronger flavor)

2 tbsp (28 g) salted butter, at room temperature

½ cup (100 g) granulated erythritol

3 large egg yolks

½ cup (123 ml) sour cream

½ tsp sugar-free vanilla extract

¼ cup (30 g) oat fiber, for dusting the rolling surface

Oil, for frying (I use avocado oil, but lard will also work)

½ cup (120 ml) almond milk (this is only for the baking option)

To prepare the donuts, in a medium bowl, whisk together the almond flour, protein powder, baking powder, xanthan gum powder, heavy cream powder (if using), salt and ground nutmeg and set it aside.

In the bowl of an electric stand mixer, beat together the butter and granulated erythritol until combined. Add the egg yolks, sour cream and vanilla extract and beat until completely combined.

Gradually add the flour mixture, beating just until the dough comes together. It will be sticky. Cover it with plastic wrap and chill it in the refrigerator for 30 minutes.

Line a large, rimmed baking sheet with parchment paper. Set it aside.

Roll the chilled dough onto a floured surface (I use oat fiber to dust the surface) until it's about ½ inch (1.3 cm) thick. Use a donut cutter or two round cutters (about 3 inches [8 cm] and 1 inch [2.5 cm], respectively) to cut out the donuts and the donut holes. It's helpful to dip the cutters in oat flour in between cutting each donut so that they don't stick to the dough. Place each donut on the parchment-lined baking sheet. Cover it with plastic wrap and chill it for about 30 more minutes.

Add enough oil to a pot so that the oil is at least 2 inches (5 cm) deep. Attach a deep-fry thermometer to the side of the pot. Heat the oil over medium heat until it reaches 320°F (160°C).

(continued)

Glaze

½ cup (60 g) sugar-free white chocolate

2 tbsp (27 g) coconut oil, divided

¼ cup (64 g) coconut butter

¼ cup (30 g) sugar-free chocolate

When the oil has come to temperature, carefully place a couple of donuts into the pot. I usually cook the donuts in batches of two or three so that I don't overcrowd the pot (which will bring down the temperature of the oil). As soon as a donut floats to the top, fry it for 40 seconds. It's helpful to use a stopwatch at first (until you get the hang of the timing). After 40 seconds, flip the donuts over and fry for 60 to 80 seconds on the other side, or until the bottom is a nice golden brown color. Flip the donuts one more time and cook for 60 to 80 more seconds, or until the other side is golden brown. Then remove the donuts to a paper towel–lined tray. Allow the donuts to cool for about 15 minutes before glazing.

To make the glaze, in a small heatproof bowl, place the white chocolate, 1 tablespoon (14 g) of the coconut oil and the coconut butter and microwave it for 1 minute on high. The chocolate will look shiny; stir it. Continue to microwave it in 20-second intervals, stirring after each, until the chocolate is totally smooth. In a separate heatproof bowl, place the other sugar-free chocolate and remaining tablespoon (14 g) of the coconut oil and microwave it until melted.

To create the marble pattern, drop 2 to 3 teaspoons (10 to 15 ml) of the darker chocolate into the white chocolate mixture. Draw a wooden skewer or spoon through the darker chocolate to make swirl patterns inside the white chocolate.

Dunk the donuts in the glaze to fully coat the tops and sides and place them on a wire rack to set. Repeat the process, redrizzling the darker chocolate in the white glaze bowl every two to three donuts.

> *Tip:* If you plan to bake the donuts rather than frying them, add ½ cup (120 ml) of almond milk to the dough right after the sour cream. Preheat the oven to 350°F (177°C). Spray two donut pans with coconut oil spray and fill each mold about two-thirds of the way. Bake the donuts for 12 minutes before glazing.

Leili's **Cinnamon Rolls**

One of the joys of baking is making a pan of sweet rolls for the family or for a special breakfast. The house smells so good, and everyone looks forward to a soft, gooey roll. You'll love my cinnamon rolls because no one will miss out on the treats—keto or not. This keto specialty is one that makes eating a celebration again!

Serves 9   Total carbs: 10 g   Net carbs: 5 g   Fat: 50 g   Protein: 25 g

Filling

1 tbsp (8 g) cinnamon

3 tbsp (42 g) granulated erythritol

3 tbsp (42 g) brown sweetener

3 tbsp (42 g) unsalted butter, at room temperature

Sweet Dough

¼ cup (50 g) oat fiber

1¼ cups (150 g) vital wheat gluten

¼ cup (50 g) almond flour

2 tbsp (29 g) heavy cream powder

2 tbsp (29 g) whey protein isolate (vanilla flavored or unflavored)

½ tsp xanthan gum

1 tsp salt

½ tsp cinnamon

Pinch of nutmeg (optional)

3 tbsp (42 g) granulated sweetener

1 tbsp (14 g) brown sweetener

1½ tbsp (14 g) instant yeast

½ cup (118 ml) macadamia milk

4 tbsp (56 g) unsalted butter

1 tbsp (15 ml) sugar-free vanilla extract

½ cup (123 ml) sour cream

1 large egg, at room temperature

To prepare the filling, mix the cinnamon, granulated erythritol and brown sweetener in a bowl. Set it aside.

To prepare the dough, in the bowl of your stand mixer, add the oat fiber, vital wheat gluten, almond flour, heavy cream powder, whey protein isolate, xanthan gum, salt, cinnamon, nutmeg (if using), granulated sweetener, brown sweetener and yeast, then whisk them together to combine. Set it aside.

In a separate bowl, add the macadamia milk, butter, vanilla extract and sour cream. Microwave them until they are warm to the touch (about 110°F [43°C]) and stir until the butter is melted.

Attach a dough hook to the mixer and pour the wet mixture into the dry mixture, then mix them together on low. Drop in the egg and mix until the dough comes together. It should be tacky but not stick to your fingers. Knead in the mixer on low speed for about 6 minutes. Cover it and allow it to rise in a warm place for 2 hours.

On a clean surface, roll out the dough to a rectangle that's ¼ inch (6 mm) thick. Spread the room temperature butter over the surface, leaving a little less than 1 inch (2.5 cm) at one of the narrow sides. If you choose the wider side for the unbuttered strip, then you'll end up with more cinnamon rolls, but they will be smaller.

Sprinkle the dough generously with the cinnamon mixture. Starting with the buttered side, roll the dough to create a long roll, ending at the unbuttered strip.

Cut the dough into 9 even pieces, each about 1½ inches (4 cm) long. You can use a length of dental floss that you loop around the roll and then pull or just use a sharp knife.

(continued)

Glaze

4 oz (112 g) cream cheese, at room temperature

2 tbsp (28 g) unsalted butter, at room temperature

1 tbsp (15 ml) sugar-free vanilla extract

Pinch of salt

1 tsp lemon juice

1 tbsp (15 ml) macadamia milk, plus more if needed for consistency

½ cup (100 g) powdered erythritol

Place the rolls cut side up in a 9 x 9–inch (23 x 23–cm) baking dish and allow them to rest in a warm place for about 40 minutes for a final rise. Make the glaze while the rolls are rising or while they are baking.

Preheat the oven to 350°F (177°C).

Bake the rolls for about 18 to 25 minutes, or until lightly browned on top. If your rolls are getting a bit too brown at the 20-minute mark, then cover them loosely with foil and continue to bake.

To make the glaze, place the cream cheese, butter, vanilla extract, salt, lemon juice and macadamia milk in a bowl and beat until smooth. (You can also make this very easily in a small food processor if you have one.) Once smooth, add the powdered erythritol and beat once more until it is fully mixed. If desired, you can thin this frosting with another 1 to 2 tablespoons (15 to 30 ml) of macadamia milk.

As soon as you remove the cinnamon rolls from the oven, drizzle about half the glaze over them. Let them cool on a wire rack, then pour the remainder of the glaze over the rolls. Enjoy!

Button Pancakes *in a Bowl*

Pancake lovers, rejoice! Here are keto pancakes in a bowl! They are so easy to make that children can do it because all the ingredients are mixed quickly in a blender. A squeeze bottle makes it easy to form the little pancakes. No one will miss the carbs in this recipe because the taste is outstanding. Another keto surprise for the whole family!

Serves 4   Total carbs: 7 g   Net carbs: 4 g   Fat: 39 g   Protein: 16 g

---

Cooking oil or butter, for greasing the pan

8 oz (227 g) cream cheese, softened at room temperature

4 eggs

1 cup (100 g) almond flour

¼ cup (50 g) granulated erythritol

½ cup (120 ml) keto-approved milk of your choice

2 tsp (10 g) baking powder

1 tsp sugar-free vanilla extract

Heat a nonstick pan or griddle over medium heat and grease it lightly with the cooking oil or butter.

Add the cream cheese, eggs, almond flour, granulated erythritol, milk, baking powder and vanilla extract to a blender and blend until the mixture is smooth. Allow the batter to rest for 5 minutes while the pan heats.

Pour the pancake batter into a squeezable condiment/sauce bottle. (Alternatively, use a zippered plastic bag, cutting a tiny hole on an angle in the bottom corner of the bag to pipe out the batter.) This will let you control the size of the pancakes more easily.

Squeeze small dots of batter onto the hot greased pan. Cook them until the tops form bubbles and look set and dry. Flip them with a spatula and cook them until they are golden on the undersides, about a further 1 to 2 minutes. Repeat with the remaining batter, lightly greasing your pan between each batch. Cook them slightly longer for a crispier pancake.

Serve the mini keto pancakes in a small bowl, adding your toppings of choice. My boys like to pour milk over the pancakes, or you can use sugar-free syrup.

Good Morning Blueberry Scones

Do you miss enjoying scones over a cup of tea? This recipe has you covered! These keto scones are soft, flaky and bursting with juicy blueberries. Topped with a creamy lemon glaze, easy scones are a recipe for a good morning.

It's just as easy to make a double batch so you have some for later. You'll be ready for drop-in company!

Serves 8   Total carbs: 9 g   Net carbs: 4 g   Fat: 20 g   Protein: 8 g

---

Scones

2 cups (200 g) almond flour

¼ cup (50 g) granulated erythritol, plus more for sprinkling

2 tbsp (15 g) coconut flour

¼ tsp cinnamon

1 tsp xanthan gum or 2 tsp (5 g) flaxseed meal

½ tsp baking soda

1 tsp baking powder

Zest of 1 lemon

¼ tsp salt

1 egg, chilled

¼ cup (60 ml) cold heavy whipping cream

2 tbsp (28 g) unsalted butter, melted and cooled, plus more for brushing the tops

1 tsp sugar-free vanilla extract

½ cup (75 g) blueberries (fresh or frozen)

Glaze

¼ cup (50 g) powdered erythritol

Zest of ½ lemon

2–3 tsp (10–15 ml) lemon juice

Preheat the oven to 350°F (177°C). Line a baking sheet with parchment paper and set it aside.

In a medium bowl, add the almond flour, granulated erythritol, coconut flour, cinnamon, xanthan gum, baking soda, baking powder, lemon zest and salt, mixing until combined.

Mix the egg, heavy whipping cream, butter and vanilla extract to the dry ingredients, mixing until combined and the dough starts to form a ball. Gently fold in the blueberries.

Transfer the dough to the parchment-lined baking sheet and shape it into a disc or circle. Flatten it slightly. Use a sharp knife to cut the circle into eight triangles. Carefully separate the triangles from each other so that they can bake evenly.

Brush the tops of each scone with melted butter and sprinkle a little sweetener on top.

Bake the scones for 25 to 30 minutes, or until the tops are brown and the center is set.

While the scones are baking, make the lemon glaze by mixing the powdered erythritol with the lemon zest and slowly adding the lemon juice as needed until the desired consistency is reached.

Remove the scones from the oven and drizzle them with the glaze. Allow them to cool, until they are well set, and enjoy!

Grab & Go Sausage Sandwich (*Sosis Bandari*)

Can fast food be delicious, satisfying and help you remain on your keto program? Yes! Look to the southern ports of Iran for the origins of this flavorful sandwich. It is popular throughout the country and will be popular in your kitchen too.

Serves 6   Total carbs: 15 g   Net carbs: 7 g   Fat: 31 g   Protein: 31 g

5 radishes, trimmed

2 tbsp (30 ml) avocado oil or ghee

1 lb (454 g) sausages

1 medium onion, sliced

3 cloves garlic, finely sliced

½ cup (50 g) sliced green bell pepper

3 tbsp (42 g) tomato paste

½ cup (120 ml) hot water

1 tbsp (10 g) turmeric

¼ tsp black pepper

½ tsp cayenne pepper (optional)

Buns, Baguettes and Mini Breads (page 62)

Fresh parsley or arugula

Pickles

Wash the radishes and cut them in half. Heat the avocado oil over medium heat and sauté the radishes for 10 minutes until they are cooked. Transfer them to a plate and set them aside.

Slice the sausages and fry them in the same oil for about 5 minutes. Remove them from the pan and drain.

Fry the onion until it is softened. After about 5 minutes, add the garlic and green bell pepper slices to the pan and cook for a few minutes more. Remove the onion, garlic and green bell pepper slices from the oil.

Add the tomato paste to the pan, then the hot water, turmeric, black pepper and cayenne pepper (if using), and let everything simmer over medium heat for about 5 minutes.

Add the radishes, sausages, onion, garlic and green bell pepper slices back to the pan and combine them.

Serve this with keto bread or use it to fill sandwich baguettes. Add some parsley or arugula and salty pickles, if you like, and enjoy!

Teatime Orange-Pecan Bread

Bursting with citrus flavors, this orange-pecan loaf is so welcome as a light bite with tea or coffee or served beside a morning omelet. You won't need to worry about the carbs with this keto-friendly recipe! Just enjoy the crunch of pecans and sweet orange glaze that make this quick bread shine. For extra orange flavor in the glaze, use the optional orange extract.

Serves 10   Total carbs: 7 g   Net carbs: 3 g   Fat: 26 g   Protein: 9 g

---

Bread

½ cup (113 g) unsalted butter, at room temperature

¾ cup (150 g) granulated erythritol

4 large eggs

½ tsp sugar-free vanilla extract

2 tbsp (12 g) orange zest

¼ cup (60 ml) orange juice

¼ cup (60 ml) full fat Greek yogurt

2½ cups (250 g) almond flour

¼ cup (30 g) coconut flour

½ tsp baking soda

2 tsp (10 g) baking powder

½ tsp salt

⅓ cup (50 g) pecans, finely chopped

Orange Glaze (Optional)

¾ cup (111 g) confectioners' sugar substitute

2 tbsp (30 ml) freshly squeezed orange juice

1 tsp orange zest

1 tsp orange extract (optional)

2 tbsp (30 ml) heavy whipping cream

Preheat the oven to 350°F (177°C). Grease a standard 9 x 5 x 3–inch (23 x 13 x 8–cm) loaf pan and set it aside.

To make the bread, in a large mixing bowl, beat together the butter and granulated erythritol until they are creamy and smooth. Beat in the eggs, one at a time, until they are fully combined. Mix in the vanilla extract, orange zest, orange juice and yogurt until they are combined.

In a separate bowl, whisk together the almond flour, coconut flour, baking soda, baking powder and salt. Add the dry mixture into the butter mixture and stir until it is mixed in well. Fold in the pecans.

Scrape the batter into the prepared pan and smooth it with an offset spatula. Tap the pan sharply on the counter to remove any air bubbles. Bake it for 55 to 60 minutes, or until a cake tester or toothpick inserted into the middle comes out clean. Remove it from the oven and let it cool for 15 minutes. Turn it out onto a wire rack to cool completely.

To make the orange glaze (if using), in a small mixing bowl whisk the confectioners' sugar substitute, orange juice, orange zest, orange extract (if using) and heavy whipping cream. Stir them together until they are fully combined. Drizzle the glaze over the cooled orange bread and serve.

Layered Berry Chia Pudding

Why shouldn't our keto foods look as nice as they taste? Refreshing and protein packed, this satisfying triple pudding treat is great for breakfast, a snack or lunchtime for kids. Sugar-free maple syrup adds just a touch of sweetness. With just three easy steps, you'll enjoy this creamy pudding and eat it without any guilt!

Serves 4   Total carbs: 19 g   Net carbs: 6 g   Fat: 14 g   Protein: 7 g

---

Creamy Vanilla Chia Pudding

1 cup (235 ml) almond or macadamia milk

¼ cup (60 ml) heavy whipping cream

3 tbsp (45 ml) sugar-free maple syrup

2 tsp (10 ml) sugar-free vanilla extract

Pinch of sea salt

6 tbsp (61 g) chia seeds

Raspberry Chia Seed Pudding

1 cup (125 g) fresh raspberries

1 tbsp (15 ml) sugar-free maple syrup

½ cup (117 ml) almond milk

2 tbsp (21 g) chia seeds

Blackberry Chia Seed Pudding

1 cup (144 g) fresh blackberries

1 tbsp (15 ml) sugar-free maple syrup

½ cup (117 ml) almond milk

2 tbsp (21 g) chia seeds

Toppings

½ cup (117 ml) whipped cream (optional)

Fresh blackberries

Fresh raspberries

Prepare three separate medium-sized bowls.

To prepare the creamy vanilla chia pudding, in the first bowl, whisk together the milk, heavy whipping cream, maple syrup, vanilla extract, sea salt and chia seeds. Set it aside.

To prepare the raspberry chia seed pudding, in the second bowl, smash the fresh raspberries with the maple syrup until they are smooth and no big pieces of raspberry remain. Add the almond milk. Stir in the chia seeds and set the bowl aside.

To prepare the blackberry chia seed pudding, in the third bowl, smash the fresh blackberries with the maple syrup until they are smooth and no big pieces of blackberry remain. Add the almond milk. Stir in the chia seeds and set the bowl aside.

Whisk the creamy vanilla chia seed pudding well one more time before covering it. Cover the other bowls as well.

Move the three bowls to the refrigerator to set for at least an hour, or up to overnight.

Once the puddings have set, either serve them directly from the bowls, layering the three puddings, or transfer them to individual-sized serving containers and store them until you are ready to serve.

To serve, top with the whipped cream (if desired) and the fresh berries. Enjoy!

Delectable Danish

Morning coffee with a Danish pastry—what a treat, but so many carbs! Not with these Danish! My Perfect Pastry Dough (page 68) makes all the difference in this keto version. You'll be so glad to have this recipe at your fingertips when you need a small treat or an afternoon pick-me-up. Creamy filling is hidden in the braided dough, peeking out after baking.

Serves 8   Total carbs: 7 g   Net carbs: 2 g   Fat: 24 g   Protein: 9 g

---

Filling

8 oz (227 g) cream cheese, softened

1 tbsp (15 ml) sour cream

½ cup (100 g) granulated erythritol

1 large egg yolk

1 tsp lemon juice

1 tsp arrowroot flour (this helps stabilize the filling)

1 tsp sugar-free vanilla extract

1 sheet Leili's Perfect Pastry Dough (page 68)

¼ cup (28 g) oat fiber, for the rollout surface

Egg Wash

1 egg yolk

1 tbsp (15 ml) heavy whipping cream

¼ cup (40 g) sliced almonds

Icing

½ cup (100 g) powdered sweetener

½ tsp sugar-free vanilla extract

3 tbsp (45 ml) heavy cream, plus more as needed for consistency

Preheat the oven to 375°F (190°C). Line a baking sheet with parchment paper.

To prepare the filling, in a small bowl, using a hand mixer, combine the cream cheese, sour cream, granulated erythritol, egg yolk, lemon juice, arrowroot and vanilla. Set it aside.

Roll out the dough into a 12 x 8–inch (30 x 20–cm) rectangle on a lightly floured piece of parchment paper or lightly floured silicone baking mat. Transfer the sheet of dough to the baking sheet.

Press the edges to even out the rectangle and seal any holes. Carefully spread the cream cheese filling down the center of the dough about 2 to 3 inches (5 to 8 cm) wide. Cut ½-inch (1.3-cm) diagonal strips from each side of the dough toward the filled center area. Fold the dough strips over the filling, alternating sides to get a braided pattern. You may have excess dough once you reach the end of the danish, so fold in the ends as best as you can. Whisk the egg yolk and heavy whipping cream together and brush it all over the dough. Then sprinkle the sliced almonds on top.

Bake the braid for 18 to 22 minutes, or until the filling is set and the braid is golden in color. Cool the braid before removing it from the baking sheet.

To prepare the icing, in a small bowl, mix together the powdered sweetener, vanilla extract and heavy cream. You may need to add more cream to get the desired consistency. Drizzle the icing over the Danish. Slice it into pieces and serve.

Tip: I strongly recommend refrigerating the shaped braid for at least 15 minutes, and up to 1 hour, before brushing it with the egg wash and baking it. Chilling sets the dough and the filling and helps the braid keep its shape in the oven.

Sweets
and Treats

Let's face it, we all look forward to dessert, no matter what was served for the main meal. That sweet tooth never goes away, but it doesn't need to cause you trouble.

Parties, holidays and special occasions are times when your keto planning might weaken without a good strategy. They're also the days when you long for a bit of nostalgia or happy memories that you want to recreate in a celebratory food centerpiece. Whether you are looking for a showstopper like the Persian Love Cake (page 128), Luscious Baklava Tart (page 139) or Leili's Tiramisu with Lady Fingers (page 122) or a family treat like Churro Cheesecake Bars (page 156) or Silky Smooth Lemon Meringue Pie (page 161), in this chapter you'll find my perfected recipes for the best keto versions. Your family and guests will be so pleased with these beautiful treats! Enjoy these international keto desserts and give your keto sweet tooth some love!

Leili's Tiramisu with Lady Fingers

Italian tiramisu meets keto here for a guilt-free dessert! Surely someone will follow you to the kitchen to ask for your secrets to this scrumptious confection. Just like a classic tiramisu, rich mascarpone filling contrasts with light cake layers made from liqueur-soaked lady fingers. Enjoy!

Serves 12   Total carbs: 8 g   Net carbs: 3 g   Fat: 26 g   Protein: 8 g

---

Lady Fingers

3 large eggs

1 egg white

¼ cup (50 g) granulated sweetener, divided

½ tsp sugar-free vanilla extract

⅔ cup (67 g) almond flour

1 tbsp (8 g) arrowroot flour

⅛ tsp salt

1 tbsp (7 g) powdered erythritol, for dusting

Mascarpone Filling

1½ cups (360 ml) heavy whipping cream

5 egg yolks

½ tsp sugar-free vanilla extract

⅓ cup (34 g) granulated erythritol

Preheat the oven to 350°F (177°C). Line a baking sheet with parchment paper.

To prepare the lady fingers, separate the eggs, placing the yolks in a large bowl and all the whites in a slightly smaller one. Whip the egg whites with an electric mixer on medium-high speed until they are fluffy. Add 2 tablespoons (25 g) of the granulated sweetener, in a slow and steady stream, while whipping. Continue to whip until the egg whites hold stiff peaks. Set the bowl aside.

Whip the egg yolks with another 2 tablespoons (25 g) of the granulated sweetener until they are pale and thick. Stir in the vanilla extract. Use a silicone spatula to gently fold in the whipped egg whites, taking care not to deflate all the air you have so carefully incorporated.

Mix the almond flour and arrowroot flour and sift them over the mixture. Add the salt and carefully fold once more until well incorporated. Pipe the batter into 3-inch (8-cm)-long lines onto the prepared baking sheet.

Dust the lady fingers with the powdered erythritol and bake them for 9 to 12 minutes, or until they are just beginning to turn golden around the edges. (Do not overbake; the lady fingers should be soft and moist.) Set them aside and let them cool while preparing the mascarpone filling.

To prepare the filling, in a cold mixing bowl, beat the heavy whipping cream until stiff peaks form, then place it in the refrigerator to chill.

Combine the egg yolks, vanilla extract and granulated erythritol in a glass bowl and whisk them over a pot of lightly boiling water for 12 minutes, until they are thick. (Use a double boiler if you have one for this step.)

Remove the bowl from the pot of water and place it on top of a bowl of ice to cool the mixture.

(continued)

Mascarpone Filling (cont.)

8 oz (227 g) mascarpone cheese

1 cup (240 ml) coffee liqueur, divided

¼ cup (25 g) cocoa powder, for dusting

Combine the cooled egg yolk mixture with the mascarpone cheese in a large mixing bowl and beat the mixture until it is smooth. Fold the whipped cream into the mascarpone cheese mixture until it is fully incorporated.

To assemble the tiramisu, line the bottom of an 8 x 8–inch (20 x 20–cm) baking dish with a layer of lady fingers. Using a pastry brush, brush half of the coffee liqueur onto the lady fingers.

Spread one-half of the mascarpone filling on top of the lady fingers and then dust them with the cocoa powder. Continue with another layer of lady fingers, brushing them with the rest of the coffee liqueur, followed by the mascarpone mixture, ending with a dusting of cocoa powder on top. Chill the tiramisu in the refrigerator for a minimum of 4 hours or overnight. Serve it chilled.

Store the tiramisu in the refrigerator, loosely covered, for up to 3 days. Do not leave it at room temperature.

Pumpkin Snickerdoodle Sandwich Cookies

My son loves spicy cookies and any cookie that can be twisted apart because he thinks he's getting extra! Adults love the combination of sweet spice and cream cheese too, and the pumpkin gives the cookie a nice texture. Because these cookies are in demand in our house, this is a recipe I'm proud to share for your keto cookie jar too.

Serves 12   Total carbs: 7 g   Net carbs: 4 g   Fat: 24 g   Protein: 12 g

Cookies

½ cup (112 g) unsalted butter, softened

¾ cup (150 g) granulated erythritol

¼ cup (50 g) brown sweetener

¼ cup (56 g) pumpkin purée

2 large eggs

½ tsp sugar-free vanilla extract

1½ cups (150 g) almond flour

¼ cup (28 g) coconut flour

¼ cup (50 g) creamy vanilla whey protein powder (or unflavored)

2 tsp (6 g) cream of tartar

½ tsp fine sea salt

1 tsp baking soda

½ tsp xanthan gum

1 tsp ground cinnamon

¼ tsp nutmeg

¼ tsp ground cloves

½ tsp allspice

1 tsp pumpkin pie spice

Cinnamon Coating

¼ cup (50 g) granulated erythritol

3 tsp (8 g) ground cinnamon

To prepare the cookies, in a large bowl add the butter, granulated erythritol and brown sweetener. Whisk the mixture briskly until it is smooth. Add in the pumpkin purée, eggs and the vanilla extract, whisking until combined.

In another bowl, stir together the almond flour, coconut flour, whey protein powder, cream of tartar, salt, baking soda, xanthan gum, cinnamon, nutmeg, cloves, allspice and pumpkin pie spice and whisk them to combine.

Add all of the dry ingredients to the wet ingredients and mix until *just* combined. Do not overmix the dough. Cover and chill the dough in the refrigerator for 1 hour.

Preheat the oven to 350°F (177°C). Line two baking sheets with parchment paper or silicone baking mats and set them aside.

To prepare the cinnamon coating, in a small mixing bowl, whisk together the granulated erythritol and the ground cinnamon.

Using a cookie scoop, make 24 balls from the chilled dough. Flatten each ball slightly and coat the cookie in the coating mixture, then place it on a baking sheet. Bake the cookies for 12 minutes and allow them to cool on the baking sheets for 10 minutes, then transfer the cookies to a wire rack to cool completely.

(continued)

Pumpkin Snickerdoodle Sandwich Cookies (cont.)

Pumpkin Cream Cheese Filling

6 oz (168 g) cream cheese, softened

2 tbsp (28 g) unsalted butter, softened

1 tbsp (7 g) pumpkin purée

½ cup (100 g) powdered erythritol

1½ tsp (8 g) pumpkin pie spice

Topping (Optional)

1 tbsp (15 ml) sugar-free caramel sauce (page 131)

2 tbsp (18 g) chopped pistachios

To make the pumpkin cream cheese filling, beat the cream cheese and butter with a mixer until smooth. Add in the pumpkin purée and mix it well. With the mixer running, slowly add the powdered erythritol a little at a time, then mix in the pumpkin pie spice. Spread or pipe the filling between two cookies to make them into miniature sandwiches.

If desired, drizzle some caramel sauce and chopped pistachios on top of your cookie sandwiches.

Persian Love Cake

This is a legendary cake made keto! Just the name is full of romance and indulgence, don't you think? There are several legends about this lovely, exotic, gorgeous cake. Some stories say a woman wants to charm a Persian prince, so she makes this cake with high-quality, expensive and aromatic ingredients and flavors like cardamom, saffron and pistachio.
Persian Love Cake is love in every bite.

Serves 12   Total carbs: 9 g   Net carbs: 4 g   Fat: 25 g   Protein: 11 g

Cake

3 cups (300 g) sifted almond flour

¼ cup (32 g) coconut flour

4 tbsp (32 g) unflavored protein powder

1 tbsp (14 g) baking powder

1 tsp ground cardamom

¼ tsp nutmeg

½ tsp salt

8 tbsp (112 g) unsalted butter, at room temperature

¼ cup (50 g) brown sweetener

⅔ cup (128 g) granulated erythritol

4 large eggs

½ cup (120 ml) full fat yogurt

Zest of 1 orange

¼ cup (60 ml) fresh orange juice

½ tsp sugar-free vanilla extract

Syrup

⅓ cup (79 ml) fresh lemon juice

⅓ cup (67 g) granulated erythritol

2 tbsp (30 ml) rose water

½ tsp ground saffron

Topping

¼ cup (25 g) pistachios, chopped

Rose petals, for garnish

Preheat the oven to 350°F (177°C). Grease and line a 9-inch (23-cm) round cake pan with parchment paper or use a non-stick Bundt pan and grease it with nonstick spray.

To prepare the cake, mix the almond flour, coconut flour, protein powder, baking powder, cardamom, nutmeg and salt in a bowl and set it aside.

Beat the butter, brown sweetener and granulated erythritol with an electric beater until they are incorporated. Add the eggs, yogurt, orange zest, orange juice and vanilla extract, beating until smooth.

Add the previously prepared flour and spices mixture and stir thoroughly. Pour the batter into the pan.

Bake the cake for 50 minutes to 1 hour, or until a skewer inserted into the center comes out clean.

Toward the end of the baking time, make the syrup. Place the lemon juice, granulated erythritol, rose water and saffron in a saucepan over medium heat. Bring the mixture to a simmer and stir to dissolve the erythritol. Simmer it for 2 minutes. Keep it warm (or reheat) for pouring.

Remove the cake from the oven and place it, still in the pan, on a wire rack. Immediately poke 30 to 40 holes all over the cake using a skewer (poke all the way through). Pour the warm syrup over the cake while it is still hot. Leave it to soak for 1 hour before removing the cake from the pan. Sprinkle the pistachios and rose petals over the cooled cake and slice it to serve.

Autumn **Pumpkin Bundt Cake**

Kick off the fall season by baking this easy and delicious keto pumpkin cake! Tempting pumpkin spice aromas will fill the house while you bake. This moist keto Bundt cake has a delicious pumpkin flavor and is topped with a drizzle of caramel sauce glaze. Allulose gives the best sweetener flavor for this cake. Guaranteed to become a family favorite, it's much easier than making pumpkin pie and is the perfect dessert for fall.

Serves 12   Total carbs: 7 g   Net carbs: 3 g   Fat: 27 g   Protein: 10 g

Cake

2½ cups (250 g) almond flour

½ cup (56 g) coconut flour

⅓ cup (30 g) unflavored whey protein

1 tbsp (14 g) baking powder

¼ tsp salt

2 tsp (5 g) ground cinnamon

¼ tsp ginger

½ tsp ground cloves

½ tsp ground nutmeg

½ tsp ground allspice

½ cup (112 g) unsalted butter, melted

5 large eggs

¼ cup (50 g) brown sweetener

¾ cup (165 g) allulose

¾ cup (168 g) pumpkin purée

½ cup (123 ml) sour cream

1 tsp sugar-free vanilla extract

¼ cup (40 g) chopped pecans (optional)

Caramel Sauce (Optional)

2 tbsp (28 g) unsalted butter

1 cup (240 ml) heavy cream

½ cup (100 g) allulose

1 tsp sugar-free vanilla extract

¼ tsp salt (optional)

Preheat the oven to 325°F (165°C). Grease a 9-inch (23-cm) Bundt pan with nonstick spray.

To prepare the cake, whisk the almond flour, coconut flour, unflavored whey protein, baking powder, salt, cinnamon, ginger, cloves, nutmeg and allspice together in a large bowl and set it aside. Whisk the melted butter, eggs, brown sweetener, allulose, pumpkin purée, sour cream and vanilla extract together until they are combined. Pour the wet ingredients into the dry ingredients and use a mixer or whisk to blend them all completely. Add the chopped pecans, if using.

Pour the batter into the greased Bundt pan. Bake the cake for 55 to 65 minutes, or until a toothpick inserted into the cake comes out clean with just a couple of lightly moist crumbs. This is a large, heavy cake, so don't be alarmed if it takes a little longer in your oven.

Once the cake is done, remove it from the oven and allow it to cool for 1 hour in the pan.

Meanwhile, make the caramel sauce, if using. Add the butter in a small saucepan or deep pot over medium heat, stirring until fully browned, about 5 minutes. Then combine the heavy cream, allulose, vanilla extract and salt (if using) and bring them to a boil over high heat, stirring constantly. Reduce the heat, and let the mixture simmer until the sauce is thick, glossy and golden brown, 5 to 7 minutes. Remove the sauce from the heat and let it cool completely.

Invert the slightly cooled cake onto a wire rack or serving dish. Allow it to cool completely, then spoon the caramel sauce over the cake.

Chocolate Caramel Cupcakes

Would you hesitate to eat a delicious-looking chocolate caramel cupcake because it would sabotage your keto diet? With these cupcakes, you don't have to! You'll find that this recipe has the perfect balance of protein and fats to give great flavor and texture to the cake, and no one will miss the carbs. Caramel frosting completes the temptation.

Serves 12   **Total carbs: 5 g**   **Net carbs: 3 g**   **Fat: 21 g**   **Protein: 5 g**

Cupcakes

1¼ cups (125 g) almond flour, sifted

¼ cup (28 g) coconut flour

⅓ cup (27 g) unsweetened natural cocoa powder, sifted

2 tsp (14 g) baking powder

½ tsp baking soda

¼ tsp salt

3 large eggs, at room temperature

½ cup (100 g) granulated erythritol

¼ cup (50 g) brown sweetener

⅓ cup (76 g) unsalted butter, ghee or coconut oil, melted

2 tsp (10 ml) sugar-free vanilla extract

¼ cup (60 ml) full fat coconut cream or heavy whipping cream, at room temperature

Frosting

2 tbsp (28 g) salted butter, softened

8 oz (227 g) cream cheese

¼ cup (60 ml) sugar-free caramel sauce (page 131)

2 tbsp (20 g) powdered erythritol

Preheat the oven to 350°F (177°C). Line a 12-well muffin pan with cupcake liners. Set it aside.

To prepare the cupcakes, whisk the almond flour, coconut flour, cocoa powder, baking powder, baking soda and salt together in a large bowl until they are thoroughly combined. Set the bowl aside. In a medium bowl, whisk the eggs, granulated erythritol, brown sweetener, melted butter and vanilla extract together until they are combined. Pour half of the wet ingredients into the dry ingredients, then half of the coconut cream. Gently whisk them together for a few seconds, then add the remainder of the wet ingredients and cream, whisking again to combine.

Pour or spoon the batter into the liners, filling each three-quarters full.

Bake the cupcakes for 20 to 25 minutes, or until a skewer inserted comes out clean. Cool them in the pan for 10 minutes, then transfer them to a wire rack. Allow the cupcakes to cool completely.

To prepare the frosting, in the bowl of a stand mixer with the paddle attachment (or using a handheld mixer), combine the butter and cream cheese until smooth and creamy, about 1 minute. Add the caramel sauce and powdered erythritol and beat them until well combined.

Transfer the frosting to a piping bag with a tip and decorate the top of each cupcake before serving.

Persian Saffron Ice Cream (*Bastani Sonnati*)

Bastani Sonnati or **Bastani Zaferooni** is a traditional Iranian ice cream made with saffron, rose water and pistachios, and it's one of the best classic Persian desserts. Making this family favorite with my mother is one of my early cooking memories that I treasure. Let's visit my mother's kitchen with this delicious keto version that your family will love too.

Serves 8   Total carbs: 4 g   Net carbs: 4 g   Fat: 30 g   Protein: 8 g

1 cup (236 ml) unsweetened almond milk

2½ cups (590 ml) heavy whipping cream, plus more for making frozen cream pieces (optional)

5 egg yolks

⅔ cup (130 g) granulated erythritol

½ tsp vegetable glycerin

1 tsp sugar-free vanilla extract

½ tsp saffron, ground and dissolved in 1 tbsp (15 ml) hot water

½ tsp cardamom powder

2 tbsp (30 ml) rose water or ¾ tsp rose extract

¼ cup (25 g) pistachio nuts, chopped (if using salted ones, soak and drain first), plus more for serving

Bring the almond milk and the heavy whipping cream to a simmer in a heavy medium saucepan. Remove it from the heat. Whisk the egg yolks in a large heatproof bowl. Add the granulated erythritol and whisk until it is blended.

Gradually whisk the hot cream mixture into the egg yolks. Be sure to add it slowly and whisk vigorously to keep the egg yolks from cooking. Return the mixture to the saucepan. Cook the mixture over low heat, stirring frequently, until it reaches a temperature of 165 to 170°F (74 to 77°C). Whisk in the glycerin, vanilla extract, saffron and cardamom powder. Cool the mixture quickly and completely, stirring occasionally, by placing the pan into a bowl of ice.

Once the pan is cold, combine the mixture with the rose water and chopped pistachios. Pour the cold mixture into an ice cream maker and freeze it according to the manufacturer's instructions. When the ice cream reaches the desired consistency, transfer it to a freezer-safe container with a lid.

Allow the ice cream to soften in the refrigerator for 10 to 15 minutes before serving with more chopped pistachios and frozen cream pieces.

Frozen Cream Pieces: Authentic Persian saffron ice cream often includes chunks of frozen cream. To make this, simply pour heavy cream in a thin layer on a flat plate that has been lined with parchment paper. Place the plate in the freezer and let the cream freeze until it is hard. Then break the cream crust into ½-inch (1.3-cm) pieces and add it along with the pistachios or just on top of the scooped ice cream. To store, place a piece of parchment paper on top of the ice cream and store it in an airtight container to prevent ice crystal formation.

Leili's Sesame Cookies

New Year's parties at my family home always featured sesame cookies. They are a beloved Middle Eastern treat—portable, versatile and not too sweet. They are great with a cup of coffee, and they are also sturdy enough to use for ice cream sandwiches. The nutty crunch of a crumbled cookie makes a nice contrast to a delicate pudding. Sesame seeds, almond flour and tahini all contribute to the protein power of this delicious keto and vegan snack I've created just for you.

Serves 12   Total carbs: 3 g   Net carbs: 1 g   Fat: 16 g   Protein: 5 g

---

1 cup (152 g) sesame seeds

¾ cup (75 g) almond flour

½ cup (100 g) granulated erythritol

4 tbsp (56 g) unsalted butter, softened

1 tbsp (16 ml) fresh-squeezed lemon juice

½ tsp baking soda

½ tsp sugar-free vanilla extract

¼ tsp salt

1 tbsp (20 g) tahini

1 large egg (see Tip)

Preheat the oven to 325°F (165°C). Line cookie sheets with parchment paper.

In a large heavy skillet over medium heat, toast the sesame seeds until they are golden brown, about 3 minutes, shaking the skillet and stirring frequently to keep them moving. Remove them from the heat and set them aside.

Place the almond flour, granulated erythritol, butter, lemon juice, baking soda, vanilla extract, salt, tahini and egg into a large mixing bowl. With an electric mixer on low speed, beat until the dough is well blended, occasionally scraping the bowl.

Fold in the sesame seeds until they are thoroughly mixed. Chill the mixture in the refrigerator for at least 30 minutes.

Divide the dough into 12 equal balls. Bake the cookies for 15 to 20 minutes, or until lightly browned.

Remove the cookies to wire racks to cool. Store the cookies in a tightly covered container for up to 1 week.

Tip: To substitute flax for the egg if needed, whisk together 1 tablespoon (9 g) of ground flaxseed and 3 tablespoons (45 ml) of warm water. Let it set for 15 minutes.

Luscious Baklava Tart

To create this recipe, I pulled ideas from numerous authentic recipes found around the world. I used combinations of Persian, Italian and Turkish baklava and also included frangipane. When I introduced this dessert to my friends from different countries, they could not resist it and said the taste is heavenly. They had no idea it was keto!

Serves 12   Total carbs: 14 g   Net carbs: 6 g   Fat: 35 g   Protein: 11 g

Tart Shell
1½ cups (150 g) almond flour

½ cup (56 g) coconut flour

5 tbsp (65 g) powdered erythritol

2 large eggs

4 tbsp (56 g) unsalted butter, cold

½ tsp sugar-free vanilla extract

Nut Filling
¾ cup (92 g) pistachios

¾ cup (84 g) hazelnuts

¼ cup (28 g) walnuts

2½ tsp (7 g) cinnamon

¼ cup (50 g) powdered sweetener

¼ tsp cardamom powder

To prepare the tart shell, preheat the oven to 350°F (177°C). Spray a 10-inch (25-cm) tart pan with a removable bottom with cooking spray.

Place the almond flour, coconut flour, powdered erythritol, eggs, butter and vanilla extract in the bowl of a food processor. Pulse them until the dough comes together. Shape the dough into a ball, wrap it in a piece of plastic wrap and refrigerate it for 30 minutes.

Once the dough is chilled, roll out the pastry between two sheets of parchment paper to about 3 to 4 millimeters thick. Remove the top sheet of paper and use the bottom sheet to help you flip the pastry over into the prepared tin, then remove the paper. Gently press the dough into all the corners and make sure the top edges are even. Prick the base all over with a fork.

Bake the tart shell for 12 minutes, or until the top and edges just begin to brown.

To prepare the nut filling, place the pistachios, hazelnuts and walnuts into the bowl of a food processor and pulse them until they are finely chopped. Add the cinnamon, powdered sweetener and cardamom and mix well. Set them aside.

(continued)

Luscious **Baklava Tart (cont.)**

Orange Syrup

¼ cup (50 g) allulose

¼ tsp xanthan gum

¼ cup (60 ml) water

¼ cup (85 g) sugar-free honey or another sugar-free sweetener (I recommend VitaFiber syrup)

Zest of 1 orange

2 tbsp (30 ml) orange juice

1 clove

⅛ tsp honey flavoring (optional)

¼ tsp saffron powder

Frangipane Filling

½ cup (100 g) granulated erythritol

½ cup (112 g) unsalted butter, softened

2 large eggs

1 tsp sugar-free vanilla extract

1 tbsp (7 g) coconut flour

1 cup (120 g) almond flour

To prepare the orange syrup, in a small saucepan, whisk together the allulose and the xanthan gum. Slowly stream in the water while continuing to whisk. Whisk in the sugar-free honey, orange zest and orange juice. Drop in the clove. Place the saucepan over low heat. Bring the mixture to a simmer, stirring occasionally. Simmer for 5 minutes, stirring frequently. Remove the pan from the heat, stir in the honey flavoring, if using, and saffron and set it aside.

Mix ⅓ cup (79 ml) of the syrup with the nut mixture, then spread this mixture over the tart shell base.

To prepare the frangipane filling, beat together the granulated erythritol and butter until they are light and fluffy. Add the eggs and vanilla extract and beat them well. Finally, mix in the coconut flour and almond flour.

Carefully spread the mixture over the top of the nut filling. Bake it for 30 to 35 minutes, turning the pan halfway through, until the tart is golden and springy on top. To prevent burning the edges of the tart, make a foil ring for the top of the pie crust.

This tart can be served warm, at room temperature or cold. Serve it with the leftover syrup on the side.

Leili's **Cream Puff**

Did you think that you would never eat a cream puff again now that you have committed to a keto lifestyle? These cream puffs are just waiting for you to try them.

Choux paste is the darling of pastries; it's either right or it's not. It's a magical combination of butter, water, flour and egg. The center should be somewhat soft while the outside is firm enough to hold a filling but not too brown. The puffs dry in the residual heat of the oven after baking to reach this consistency. After much testing, I can present to you my victory—keto choux paste! I wish I could serve them to you at my table! They'll be the star at your table for sure, and you can be sure that your keto baking secrets will be hidden in the perfect taste and texture. *Bon appétit!*

Yields 18 cream puffs   Total carbs: 4 g   Net carbs: 2 g   Fat: 13 g   Protein: 8 g

---

Pastry Puff

¾ cup (96 g) vital wheat gluten, sifted

1 tbsp (3 g) oat fiber

¼ cup (24 g) unflavored whey protein

1 tbsp (8 g) arrowroot flour

½ tsp xanthan gum

1½ tsp (7 g) baking powder

½ cup (118 ml) water

⅓ cup (78 ml) almond milk or macadamia milk

1 stick (112 g) unsalted butter, cut into 8 pieces

½ tsp salt

¼ tsp sugar-free vanilla extract

1 tbsp (15 g) granulated erythritol

4 eggs, beaten

Preheat the oven to 350°F (177°C).

To prepare the pastry puffs, in a medium bowl, whisk together the vital wheat gluten, oat fiber, whey protein, arrowroot, xanthan gum and baking powder and set it aside.

Put the water, almond milk, butter, salt, vanilla extract and granulated erythritol into a small saucepan and heat it on medium heat until the butter melts and the liquid comes to a full boil. Take it off the heat. Immediately add all the flour at once and stir it vigorously with a spoon or spatula until all the flour is incorporated and the flour lumps are smoothed out. Put the saucepan back over medium heat and cook, stirring constantly, for 5 minutes.

Fit the stand mixer with a paddle attachment or a hand mixer with spiral hooks. Place the dough in the mixer bowl and let it cool for 5 minutes, turning the mixer briefly on low speed for a few seconds a few times to release the steam. Turn the mixer on medium-low speed and pour in roughly a quarter of the eggs. The dough will break and gradually become creamy again. Keep adding the eggs in three more additions, waiting for the mixture to smooth out before each addition. Scrape down the bowl and beat the mixture on medium speed for about 30 seconds or until the dough is completely smooth and everything is mixed evenly.

(continued)

Cream Filling and Garnish

2 cups (470 ml) heavy whipping cream, chilled

4 tbsp (50 g) powdered erythritol, plus 1 tbsp (14 g) for garnish

1 tsp sugar-free vanilla extract

Raspberries (optional)

Move the dough into a pastry bag fitted with a ½-inch (1.3-cm) round tip. Invert an 18 x 13–inch (45 x 33–cm) half sheet pan. Dab the sheet with dough in the corners and then put the parchment paper on top so it sticks.

Pipe 18 puffs on the sheet for medium puffs. Spray the puffs with water. Dab up the tails with a wet finger to make a small peak at the top of the puff. Fill one small pan with 1 inch (2.5 cm) of boiling water and place it on the bottom of the oven. Place the baking sheet in the oven. Turn on the convection fan if you have one. Bake the puffs for 25 minutes for medium puffs before opening the oven door. Peek to see if the puffs are brown. If not, shut the door immediately. When the puffs are brown and completely firm to the touch, remove them from the oven.

Turn off the oven and carefully remove the pan of water.

If filling from the top, poke the sides of the puffs with a skewer to release the steam. If filling from the bottom, make a hole in the bottom of each puff with the empty pastry tip and wiggle in the skewer to make sure the webs of dough won't block the cream. Return the puffs to the turned off oven (with the holes facing up) for 10 minutes. Then transfer the puffs to a wire rack to cool for 5 minutes.

To prepare the cream filling and garnish, in a large mixing bowl, combine the heavy whipping cream, powdered erythritol and vanilla extract. Beat them together on medium-high speed until fluffy stiff peaks form, about 2 minutes.

Once the cream puffs are completely cooled, fill them with the cream. There are two ways to fill them: pipe the cream into the puffs by pushing the pastry tip into the bottom and piping until cream pushes back or cut off the tops of the puffs and pipe the cream into the center using a pastry bag, push a raspberry down into the center if desired, then cover with the tops. Dust the puffs with powdered sweetener and serve.

The cream puffs can be stored in the refrigerator for 24 hours after filling. Unfilled puffs can be frozen in a ziplock bag for later use. Defrost the frozen puffs for 30 minutes and recrisp them in a 350°F (177°C) oven for 5 minutes.

Lemon—Vanilla Madeleines

Madeleines are a fixture of French patisseries. The little shell-shaped cakes have charmed writers like Proust, cooks like Julia Child and many people who've enjoyed them with a cup of tea. If you've never eaten a madeleine, they are buttery little cakes with touches of almond, vanilla and lemon. You'll need a special madeleine pan, but it's well worth it for this keto recipe!
Put the kettle on for tea!

Serves 12   Total carbs: 2 g   Net carbs: 1 g   Fat: 10 g   Protein: 5 g

Madeleines

3 eggs, plus 1 egg yolk

½ cup (100 g) granulated erythritol

1 tsp vanilla bean paste or sugar-free vanilla extract

Zest of 1 lemon

1 tsp lemon juice

½ cup (50 g) almond flour, sifted

¼ cup (30 g) coconut flour, sifted

¼ cup (25 g) creamy vanilla protein powder

Pinch of salt

¼ tsp baking powder

10 tbsp (140 g) unsalted butter, melted and cooled

Lemon Icing Glaze (Optional)

¾ cup (135 g) powdered erythritol

3 tbsp (45 ml) freshly squeezed lemon juice

2 tsp (4 g) lemon zest

2 tbsp (30 ml) heavy whipping cream

Preheat the oven to 350°F (177°C).

To prepare the madeleines, in a medium bowl, beat the eggs with an electric hand mixer until they are pale yellow and fluffy, 2 to 3 minutes. Add the granulated erythritol and blend. Add the vanilla bean paste, lemon zest and lemon juice and blend again.

In a separate bowl, sift together the almond flour, coconut flour, protein powder, salt and baking powder. Add the flour mixture to the batter and gently fold it in by hand.

Slowly pour in the melted butter and fold the batter gently by hand until everything is completely incorporated. Let it rest for 20 minutes.

Spray the madeleine tray with oil and place 1 tablespoon (15 ml) of the mixture into each shell. Do not overfill it. Bake the madeleines for 8 to 12 minutes, or until cooked through and golden on top. Remove them from the oven and allow them to cool completely on the pan.

Meanwhile, to make the optional lemon icing, whisk the powdered erythritol, lemon juice, lemon zest and heavy whipping cream in a small bowl and stir until fully combined.

Spoon the icing over the madeleines or dip half of each madeleine in the glaze. Let them stand for at least 5 minutes to set the glaze before serving.

Triple—Layered Heavenly Panna Cotta

A deceptively easy Italian dessert, panna cotta will become one of your go-to beautiful creations as well as a family favorite. My keto version layers saffron, vanilla and pistachio ganache for a delightful combination of flavors in alternating layers. Your guests will lick their spoons to get the last bit of delicious panna cotta. This is one to share proudly!

Serves 6   Total carbs: 6 g   Net carbs: 5 g   Fat: 35 g   Protein: 10 g

Panna Cotta

1½ tbsp (14 g) gelatin powder

¼ cup (59 ml) cold water

2 cups (470 ml) heavy whipping cream

1 cup (235 ml) unsweetened almond milk

⅔ cup (67 g) granulated erythritol

1 tsp sugar-free vanilla extract, divided

1 tsp ground cardamom

2 tbsp (30 ml) rose water

¼ tsp saffron, ground and dissolved in 1 tbsp (15 ml) hot water

Chopped pistachios and whipped cream, for topping

Pistachio Ganache

½ cup (120 ml) heavy cream

¼ cup (40 g) white chocolate, chopped

3 tbsp (51 g) pistachio powder

2 tsp (16 g) powdered sweetener, sifted (optional)

⅛ tsp fine sea salt

⅛ tsp cardamom

⅛ tsp vanilla powder (optional)

To prepare the panna cotta, in a small bowl, sprinkle the gelatin powder over the cold water and let it stand for about 5 minutes.

Meanwhile, combine the heavy whipping cream, almond milk and granulated erythritol in a small saucepan. Heat it over medium heat, stirring until the erythritol is fully dissolved, about 5 minutes. Add the gelatin to the cream mixture, stirring vigorously until well combined. Remove the saucepan from the heat.

To make the vanilla-flavored layer, pour one-half of the mixture into another bowl and add ½ teaspoon of the vanilla extract. Whisk them together.

To make the saffron-flavored layer, pour the second half of the mixture into another bowl and add the other ½ teaspoon of vanilla extract, the ground cardamom, rose water and saffron water. Whisk them together until thoroughly incorporated.

To make a layered panna cotta, begin by filling small bowls with dry rice to anchor the glasses while you pour. Place the serving glasses in the bowls at a tilted angle. Pour in your first layer of panna cotta and chill it in the refrigerator, tilted, for at least 30 minutes or until the layer is set. Turn the glass to a different angle (optional), pour in the second layer and chill again. Repeat and alternate the saffron and vanilla layers as desired. Of course, you can also fill the serving glasses with horizontal layers of panna cotta if you desire.

While the panna cotta is firming, make the pistachio ganache. In a small microwave-safe bowl, microwave the heavy cream for 45 seconds. Remove it from the microwave, then stir in the white chocolate, pistachio powder, powdered sweetener (if using), sea salt, cardamom and vanilla powder (if using) until smooth.

Pour the ganache over the set panna cotta just before serving. Garnish with chopped pistachios and whipped cream and enjoy!

Nutty Treasure Bites

Some protein is more fun than others! These are the treasures I hide for myself. Perfect with a strong cup of coffee, they feel so decadent but are full of healthy nuts and fats with an extra load of flavor from hazelnuts and coconut cream. These little gems are great on a cookie tray and also make a nice after school snack. Here's a keto treat to really enjoy!

Serves 10   Total carbs: 10 g   Net carbs: 5 g   Fat: 35 g   Protein: 10 g

---

Crème Layer

½ cup (43 g) hazelnuts

¾ cup (171 g) coconut cream

¼ cup (59 ml) sugar-free maple syrup

⅓ cup (78 ml) almond milk

⅓ cup (80 g) peanut butter

⅓ cup (70 g) coconut oil, melted

½ cup (50 g) almond flour

⅓ cup (130 g) peanut butter powder

Caramel Layer

¼ cup (59 ml) Sukrin Fiber Syrup Gold

⅓ cup (78 ml) sugar-free maple syrup

⅔ cup (160 g) tahini (unsalted)

⅛ tsp salt

1 tbsp (14 g) coconut oil

½ cup (73 g) salted peanuts

Chocolate Coating

8 oz (227 g) stevia sweetened chocolate chips

1–2 tbsp (14–27 g) coconut oil

2 tbsp (30 ml) sugar-free maple syrup (optional)

Line an 8 x 8–inch (20 x 20–cm) pan with parchment paper or plastic wrap, extending it beyond the edges of the pan for easy removal later.

To prepare the crème layer, in a food processor or high-speed blender, combine the hazelnuts, coconut cream, sugar-free maple syrup, almond milk, peanut butter and coconut oil. Process this mixture until it is completely smooth for 5 to 10 minutes. Transfer the hazelnut peanut butter mixture into a medium-sized bowl. Add the almond flour and peanut butter powder and combine them well.

Pour this mixture into the pan and freeze it for 50 to 60 minutes.

In the meantime, prepare the caramel layer. In a small saucepan, combine the Sukrin Fiber Syrup Gold, maple syrup, tahini, salt and coconut oil. Combine them and stir over low heat until the mixture is smooth. Remove it from the heat and fold in the peanuts.

Pour the caramel sauce with the peanuts on top of the frozen peanut butter mixture and freeze it for another 60 minutes.

To prepare the chocolate coating, in a small saucepan, combine the chocolate chips, coconut oil and sugar-free maple syrup (optional). Stir this mixture over low heat until it is combined and smooth.

Run a knife along the edges of the pan to loosen the bars. Using the edges of the parchment paper, lift the bars out of the pan onto a cutting board and cut them into 10 sections. Dip the frozen bars into the melted chocolate and transfer them to a wire rack until the chocolate sets.

Enjoy the bars immediately or store them in an airtight container in the fridge for up to 2 weeks.

Peter Rabbit's **Cheesecake**

Little Peter Rabbit could not resist the carrots in Mr. McGregor's garden, and you will find it hard to resist this combination dessert! A delight for the senses, it's a perfect moist keto carrot cake plus a perfect keto lemon cheesecake. Do you suspect that these stunning layers are full of carbs? Surprise, this keto success is something everyone will enjoy. Prepare this dessert the day before you plan to serve it.

Serves 12   Total carbs: 6 g   Net carbs: 4 g   Fat: 38 g   Protein: 9 g

Cheesecake Mixture

½ cup (100 g) granulated sweetener

1 tsp xanthan gum

16 oz (454 g) cream cheese, softened

2 large eggs

1 tsp sugar-free vanilla extract

½ cup (123 ml) sour cream

Carrot Cake

1½ cups (150 g) almond flour

¼ cup (31 g) coconut flour

½ tsp baking soda

1 tsp baking powder

¼ tsp salt

1 tsp ground cinnamon

⅛ tsp ground nutmeg

½ cup (112 g) unsalted butter, melted

¼ cup (60 ml) unsweetened almond milk

⅓ cup (66 g) granulated erythritol

¼ cup (50 g) brown sweetener

2 large eggs

1 tsp sugar-free vanilla extract

1 cup (110 g) finely grated carrots

¼ cup (25 g) chopped walnuts (optional)

Preheat the oven to 350°F (177°C). Butter a 9-inch (23-cm) springform pan and set it aside.

To prepare the cheesecake mixture, in a mixing bowl, whisk together the granulated sweetener and the xanthan gum until they are well combined. Add the cream cheese and, using an electric hand mixer set on low speed, blend the mixture together until it is smooth.

Mix in the eggs one at a time, mixing just until combined after each addition and adding in the vanilla extract with the second egg. Blend in the sour cream. Forcefully tap the bowl against the countertop to release any air bubbles. Set the mixture aside.

To prepare the carrot cake, in a medium mixing bowl, whisk together the almond flour, coconut flour, baking soda, baking powder, salt, cinnamon and nutmeg until they are blended.

In a separate large mixing bowl, add the melted butter, almond milk, granulated erythritol, brown sweetener, eggs and vanilla extract and blend the mixture using an electric hand mixer set on low speed for 1 minute.

With the mixer running on low speed, slowly add in the dry ingredients and mix until they are well blended. Add the carrots and chopped walnuts (if using) and mix until they are evenly distributed. Tap the bowl forcefully against the counter to release any large air pockets.

(continued)

Topping

3 oz (85 g) cream cheese, softened

1 tbsp (14 g) unsalted butter, softened

½ cup (100 g) powdered erythritol

¼ cup (60 ml) sour cream

½ tsp sugar-free vanilla extract

⅓ cup (33 g) chopped pecans or walnuts (optional)

To assemble the cheesecake, pour one-third of the carrot cake mixture into the buttered springform pan and spread it into an even layer. Dollop about one-third of the cheesecake mixture by the spoonful over the carrot cake layer.

Spoon the remaining carrot cake mixture over the cheesecake layer, then finish by drizzling the remaining cheesecake mixture over the carrot cake layer, working to cover all of the carrot cake mixture.

Bake the cheesecake for 60 to 65 minutes, or until the center portion only jiggles slightly. When the cheesecake is done baking, turn off the oven, leave the cheesecake on the oven rack and prop the door open a few inches for another hour. This will keep the cheesecake from cracking or sinking. Remove the cake from the oven and allow it to cool on a wire rack for 1 hour, then cover it with foil and chill it in the refrigerator for 6 hours or overnight.

For the topping, in a mixing bowl, using an electric hand mixer, whip together the cream cheese and butter until they are smooth. Add the powdered erythritol, sour cream and vanilla extract and mix them until they are fluffy, 4 to 5 minutes.

Spread the frosting evenly over the top and sides of the cheesecake. Decorate the cheesecake with chopped pecans or walnuts (if using). Store it in the refrigerator in an airtight container for up to 7 days.

Tempting **Pecan Pie Cheesecake**

So hard to decide—do I want to make cheesecake for my holiday dessert or pecan pie? My family and friends love both, and I've got the keto techniques that make both work well. This combination is a great success for you and your guests. Creamy, sweet, crunchy, spectacular on the plate—and low carb! Just what everyone wants! Before you get started, be sure to allow enough time for the process. While the steps in this recipe are not hard, they require time. I like to start this cheesecake about 36 hours before I plan to serve it.

Serves 16   Total carbs: 9 g   Net carbs: 4.3 g   Fat: 44 g   Protein: 8.6 g

Crust

1 cup (100 g) ground pecans

1 cup (100 g) almond flour

4 tbsp (32 g) coconut flour

¼ cup (50 g) granulated erythritol

½ tbsp (4 g) cinnamon

4 tbsp (56 g) unsalted butter, melted

½ tsp sugar-free vanilla extract

Cheesecake Filling

24 oz (672 g) cream cheese, softened and at room temperature

1 cup (200 g) granulated erythritol

¼ cup (60 ml) heavy whipping cream

½ cup (123 ml) sour cream, at room temperature

1 tbsp (15 ml) sugar-free vanilla extract

1 tsp baking powder

1 tsp cinnamon

¼ tsp salt

3 large eggs, at room temperature, lightly beaten, plus 1 egg yolk

Preheat the oven to 320°F (160°C) fan assisted or 350°F (177°C) conventional.

To prepare the crust, line a 9-inch (23-cm) springform pan. To do this, cut a piece of parchment paper slightly larger than the base, place it over the base, then position and lock the sides of the pan into place over the parchment paper to hold it there. Then wrap the whole base in aluminum foil that comes up the sides almost to the top. This is an important step for later when you bake the cheesecake in a bigger, deeper pan to make a water bath.

Combine the ground pecans, almond flour, coconut flour, granulated erythritol and cinnamon in a food processor. Mix in the butter and sugar-free vanilla extract. Pour the crust mixture into the lined springform pan and press it halfway up the sides, using your fingers or a flat-bottomed cup to press the mixture into the bottom. Refrigerate the crust for 20 minutes.

For the cheesecake filling, beat the cream cheese and granulated erythritol with an electric mixer on medium-high speed until they are smooth and creamy. Add the heavy whipping cream, sour cream, vanilla extract, baking powder, cinnamon and salt. Beat them until the mixture is well combined, then beat in the eggs, being careful not to mix at too high a speed—add the eggs at low speed, then continue at medium speed until it is well mixed but not bubbly. Do not mix on high speed!

Pour the cheesecake filling through a fine-mesh sieve into the cake pan to remove any large lumps. Use an offset spatula to spread the batter evenly in the pan.

(continued)

Pecan Pie Topping

⅓ cup (53 g) brown sugar substitute

4 tbsp (60 ml) sugar-free maple syrup

1 tsp xanthan gum or glucomannan powder

½ cup (112 g) unsalted butter

2 large eggs

¼ tsp sea salt

½ cup (120 ml) heavy whipping cream

2 cups (218 g) pecans, coarsely chopped

Use a water bath to bake the cheesecake. Set the filled springform pan into a deep baking pan first, then fill the outer pan with 1 inch (2.5 cm) or so of hot water. Do not overfill. Be sure the springform pan is protected from the hot water. The hot moist air in the oven will keep the surface of the cheesecake from hardening too soon, and the hot water will provide an even temperature for baking the filling.

Bake the cheesecake for 40 minutes. Don't peek until the 40 minutes are up and do not touch the cheesecake or try to insert anything to test the filling. The top should be just golden brown.

Once the cheesecake goes into the oven, begin working on the pecan pie topping. Combine the brown sugar substitute, maple syrup, xanthan gum and butter in a medium saucepan. Cook the mixture over medium heat until it reaches a boil, stirring constantly. Continue to boil it for 2 minutes. Remove it from the heat and let it cool while the cheesecake is baking.

Meanwhile, whisk the eggs, salt and heavy whipping cream together. Set it aside. Slowly whisk the egg mixture with the cooled syrup until well combined. Stir in the chopped pecans

After the cheesecake has baked for 40 minutes, remove it from the oven and lower the oven temperature to 300°F (150°C).

Carefully spoon the pecan pie topping mixture over the cheesecake and return it to the oven to continue baking at the reduced temperature for another 40 to 50 minutes, until the top is golden brown and crisp. (If the edges of the pecan topping are browning during baking, cover them with foil.)

When the cheesecake is done baking, turn off the oven, leave the cheesecake on the oven rack and prop the door open a few inches for another hour. This is the start of the gradual cooling that will keep the cheesecake from cracking or sinking.

Remove the cheesecake from the oven after 1 hour and allow the cheesecake to cool gradually on a wire rack on the counter for 2 hours. Then cover it with a towel or paper towel and chill it in the refrigerator. You can enjoy the cheesecake after a few hours of chilling, but it's much easier to cut if you've chilled it overnight. Run a knife around the edge of the cake before releasing it from the pan.

Churro Cheesecake Bars

Two fabulous desserts in one! Simple ingredients combine to make this layered dessert interesting, easy and keto friendly. Who doesn't love a little cheesecake, especially when it's nestled in flaky pastry and dusted with cinnamon sugar? This makes a fast dessert if you've got some of my Perfect Pastry Dough (page 68) made ahead for occasions like this. Here's a recipe you'll have to try for yourself!

Serves 9   Total carbs: 13 g   Net carbs: 3 g   Fat: 47 g   Protein: 16 g

---

16 oz (454 g) cream cheese, softened

1 cup (200 g) granulated erythritol, divided

2 eggs, at room temperature

¼ cup (60 g) sour cream

1 tsp sugar-free vanilla extract

½ cup (112 g) unsalted butter, melted

2 tbsp (16 g) ground cinnamon

2 sheets Leili's Perfect Pastry Dough (page 68)

Preheat the oven to 350°F (177°C).

Spray a 9 x 9–inch (23 x 23–cm) baking pan with nonstick spray and line it with parchment paper. Set it aside.

In a large mixing bowl, combine the cream cheese, ½ cup (100 g) of granulated erythritol, eggs, sour cream and vanilla extract. Stir them until combined and smooth and set the bowl aside.

In a small bowl, mix together the remaining ½ cup (100 g) of granulated erythritol, melted butter and cinnamon. Whisk them to combine. Set this mixture aside.

On a clean surface, roll out the dough and divide it into two flat 9 x 9–inch (23 x 23–cm) sheets.

Pour half of the cinnamon butter mixture into the bottom of the pan. Lay one sheet of dough into the bottom of the pan on top of the cinnamon butter mixture. Spread the cream cheese mixture evenly over the dough. Place the second sheet of dough on top of the cream cheese filling. Pour the remaining cinnamon butter mixture evenly over the top.

Bake the bars for 20 to 25 minutes, or until the pastry appears set. Cover it with foil halfway through the baking time.

Cool the bars and allow them to set for 30 minutes. To make cutting easy, refrigerate the bars for about 1 hour.

Tiramisu **Cheesecake**

Mmm, cheesecake! Mmm, tiramisu! How can such a yummy dessert be keto? Here's a recipe to delight and intrigue everyone. Your keto baking skills will really shine in this sophisticated creation, and all will enjoy!

Serves 16   Total carbs: 5 g   Net carbs: 3 g   Fat: 37 g   Protein: 10 g

Tiramisu Custard

4 egg yolks

3 tbsp (43 g) granulated erythritol

1 tsp sugar-free vanilla extract

8 oz (227 g) mascarpone cheese

1 cup (240 ml) whipped cream

Crust

1½ cups (150 g) almond flour

¼ cup (25 g) macadamia flour

¼ cup (50 g) granulated erythritol

4 tbsp (56 g) unsalted butter, melted

1 tsp sugar-free vanilla extract

To make the tiramisu custard, place the egg yolks, granulated erythritol and vanilla extract into a heat-resistant bowl. Beat the mixture until it is pale and creamy. Place the bowl on top of a saucepan with simmering water; the water should not touch the bowl. Reduce the heat and cook the mixture for 5 to 7 minutes, stirring constantly, until the mixture is lighter in color, increased in volume and a little frothy.

Take the bowl off the heat. Add the mascarpone to the whipped yolks and whisk them until they are smooth.

Gently fold the mascarpone and yolk mixture into the whipped cream. Transfer the mixture to the refrigerator to keep it cool.

Adjust the oven rack to the middle placement. Preheat the oven to 325°F (165°C).

To prepare the crust, line a 9-inch (23-cm) springform pan. To do this, cut a piece of parchment paper slightly larger than the base, place it over the base then position and lock the sides of the pan into place over the parchment paper to hold it there. Then wrap the whole base in aluminum foil that comes up the sides almost to the top. This is an important step for later when you bake the cheesecake in a bigger, deeper pan to make a water bath.

To make the crust, combine the almond flour, macadamia flour and granulated erythritol in a food processor. Mix in the butter and vanilla extract. Pour the crust mixture into the prepared springform pan, using a flat-bottomed cup to press the mixture into the bottom. Refrigerate the crust for 20 minutes.

(continued)

Filling

20 oz (560 g) full fat cream cheese, at room temperature

½ cup (100 g) powdered erythritol

¼ cup (50 g) brown sweetener

½ cup (120 ml) sour cream

¼ cup (60 ml) heavy cream

2 tsp (10 ml) sugar-free vanilla extract

¼ cup (25 g) creamy vanilla protein powder

1 tsp xanthan gum

1 tsp baking powder

2 tbsp (20 g) instant coffee

¼ tsp salt

4 eggs, plus 1 egg yolk

10 drops liquid sweetener

2 tbsp (15 g) cocoa powder, for dusting

To make the filling, beat the cream cheese, powdered erythritol and brown sweetener in a large bowl with an electric mixer on medium speed until they are smooth and creamy.

Add the sour cream, heavy cream, vanilla extract, protein powder, xanthan gum, baking powder, instant coffee and salt. Beat in the eggs and liquid sweetener until they are combined.

Pour the cheesecake batter into the crust.

Use a water bath to bake the cheesecake. Place the springform pan inside another larger pan. Fill the outside pan with enough warm water to go about halfway up the sides of the springform pan. The water should not go above the top edge of the aluminum foil on the springform pan.

Bake the cheesecake for 1 hour. The center should be set but still jiggly.

Turn off the oven and leave the door closed for 30 minutes. The cheesecake will continue to cook but slowly begin to cool as well.

Crack the door of the oven for 30 minutes to allow the cheesecake to continue to cool slowly. This process helps to prevent cracking.

Remove the cheesecake from the oven. At this point the cheesecake can be removed from the water bath and the wrapping removed from the pan.

Refrigerate the cheesecake until completely cool and firm, 2 to 3 hours. When the cheesecake is cool and firm, remove it from the springform pan, dust the top with cocoa powder and then add the tiramisu custard. Finally, dust with a last layer of cocoa powder.

Refrigerate the tiramisu cheesecake overnight, then serve it proudly!

Silky Smooth Lemon Meringue Pie

Perfection in a crust! Enjoy the smooth lemon filling with a balance of sweet and tart flavors, complemented by the nutty crust.

The key to this lemon meringue pie is the Italian meringue, adapted for keto use. Allulose sweetener is the secret in the filling and meringue! Because the egg whites start cooking when the boiling syrup is slowly poured into the bowl, you can be sure that they are both sturdy and safe. The result will be a glorious crown of meringue with a barely browned top after its short oven time. This pie will have everyone looking for seconds!

Serves 8   Total carbs: 6 g   Net carbs: 3 g   Fat: 22 g   Protein: 9 g

---

Crust
¼ cup (32 g) hazelnuts or pecans

1 cup (100 g) almond flour

¼ cup (32 g) slivered almonds (optional)

⅓ cup (67 g) powdered erythritol

½ tsp sugar-free vanilla extract

2 tbsp (28 g) unsalted butter, melted

Filling
1 cup (200 g) allulose

1 tbsp (9.25 g) unflavored gelatin

¼ tsp salt

1 tsp arrowroot flour

1¼ cups (296 ml) water

5 large egg yolks

½ cup (120 ml) lemon juice

4 tbsp (56 g) unsalted butter

1 tbsp (6 g) lemon zest

½ tsp sugar-free vanilla extract

Preheat the oven to 350°F (177°C).

To prepare the crust, use a food processor to combine and pulse the hazelnuts, almond flour, slivered almonds (if using), powdered erythritol, vanilla extract and butter. Press the crust into your pie pan and refrigerate it until it is firm.

To prepare the filling, combine the allulose, gelatin, salt, arrowroot and water in a saucepan and bring it to a boil while stirring constantly for 1 minute. In a small bowl, beat the egg yolks, then pour some of the gelatin mixture into the beaten yolks. Stir and pour this mixture back into the saucepan to cook until it has thickened, about 3 to 5 minutes. Do not allow the mixture to go above 160°F (71°C). Whisk the lemon juice, butter, lemon zest and vanilla extract into the egg mixture and then remove the saucepan from the heat. Whisk the mixture until the butter has melted completely and is fully incorporated.

Pour the lemon filling into the prepared pie crust.

(continued)

Italian Meringue

1½ cups (300 g) allulose

¼ cup (60 ml) water

5 large egg whites, at room temperature

¼ tsp cream of tartar

Pinch of salt

1 tsp sugar-free vanilla extract

To prepare the Italian meringue, combine the allulose and water in a small saucepan and bring them to a boil. Boil to the soft ball stage (235°F [110°C]), using a candy thermometer for accuracy. (The mixture will form a soft ball when a small amount is dropped into cold water.)

Beat the egg whites in a large bowl with the electric mixer until they are frothy. Add the cream of tartar and salt and continue beating them until soft peaks form. Very slowly, while beating vigorously, pour the hot syrup in a very thin stream over the beaten whites. Beat them until the whites are stiff and glossy, 8 to 9 minutes for stiff peaks. Add the vanilla extract toward the end of mixing. Use the meringue immediately.

Spread the meringue over the lemon filling, making sure to seal the edges, and pile more meringue in the center, swirling the meringue with a spoon or offset spatula. Bake the pie for 25 to 30 minutes, or until the meringue is browned on top. Remove the pie from the oven, place it on a wire rack and allow it to cool at room temperature for 1 hour before transferring it to the refrigerator to chill. Chill the pie in the refrigerator for 4 hours before slicing and serving.

Basics, Tools,
Tips and Tricks

This section is all about how you can preserve flavor, texture and nutrition while limiting carbs. I want you to be successful on your keto journey, so along with the recipes, I'm sharing all the tips and information about ingredients and substitutions that I've learned over the years.

In my kitchen "laboratory," I have been testing and experimenting with many kinds of substitutes for the carbohydrates that we love but are trying to avoid. I've listed my favorites in this section, and you can see from the bread and pastry recipes that even the substitutions have different uses.

I've been adapting recipes to use substitutes for wheat flour for years and have experimented with products that have some but not all of wheat's features. You need bulk, spring, structure, flavor and the right ratio of liquids to solids to get this right. Sweeteners are part of the story too. I've listed my favorites here and am always looking for new products that are more like sugar and wheat without the carbs.

The Keto Pantry: Ingredients and Tools

Vital wheat gluten is high in protein and low in carbs. It does not contain the carbs you find in wheat flour. It's just the gluten by itself. It can also give keto breads and keto baked goods the texture that makes them taste close to the real thing.

Oat fiber increases water absorption, which further helps to reduce calories; this insoluble fiber is not broken down in the body, so it is low carb. Flour made from finely ground oat fiber is useful for dusting rolling surfaces without adding extra carbs.

Lupin flour is high-protein, high-fiber flour made from a legume, the lupin bean, related to peanuts and soybeans.

Almond flour is low carb and high fat. The amount of net carbs may vary by brand, so read the labels carefully. It may be more expensive than other nut flours but has good nutrition.

Coconut flour absorbs more liquid than almond flour, is lower in fat and slightly higher in carbohydrates. A small amount is often used in recipes that contain almond flour.

Whey protein isolate is used in baking for its emulsifying, foaming, gelling, stabilizing and nutritional properties. I recommend Isopure Whey Protein Isolate.

Golden flaxseed meal is a high-protein, high-fat flour with a nutty flavor.

Wheat protein isolate 5000 is a high-protein, low-carbohydrate powder that is used to strengthen doughs. It does contain wheat gluten.

Arrowroot flour is a gluten-free, grain-free powder made from a tropical tuber. It is used in small amounts to thicken liquids and sauces and is sometimes used as a substitute for cornstarch. It is used in such small amounts that it does not affect the carb content of a dish.

Baking yeast is used to make the doughs rise. I prefer SAF granular yeast. If you bake infrequently, buy it in the small envelopes so it is fresh when you need it, but it is also available in a larger bag that should be stored in the refrigerator and used quickly. I also recommend proofing both instant (rapid rise) and active dry yeast. Sprinkle the yeast in warm water with a little sugar or honey to feed it, and you should see activity within five minutes if it is viable. Yeast is a living organism and should be treated carefully, but it gives such good results when it is pampered!

Nutritional yeast is deactivated yeast sold in flakes, granules or powder. It is full of fiber and protein, is a source of B vitamins and has a nutty or cheesy flavor. It is often used in vegetarian dishes.

Heavy cream powder adds fat and creaminess without extra liquid.

Kosher salt is salt without impurities. I recommend using the larger granules for bread baking.

Peanut butter powder has most of the fat removed from the roasted and pressed peanuts and has 70 percent less fat than peanut butter.

Pomegranate molasses is available in most supermarkets and online. Made from concentrated pomegranate juice, it adds a complex acidity and musky flavor without a sweet taste.

Binding Agents

Xanthan gum is a product of fermentation that is used in small amounts to help thicken and stabilize baked goods that are made with gluten-free flours.

Gelatin is a protein, usually made from animal collagen, that is used to thicken liquids. There is also a vegetarian form of gelatin called agar-agar that is derived from seaweed. Gelatin is sold in dried form, in sheets or powder, and must be rehydrated as the first step when used in recipes.

Dough conditioner or enhancer is an ingredient used to help with consistency and rolling. Some dough conditioners also improve texture, help with rising and enhance browning. Very little is needed to help alternative flours work better. Online baking suppliers carry this as well as some grocery stores.

Glycerin is a sugar alcohol. It can be derived from animal sources or from soy, coconut or palm oils. It is used in frozen foods to prevent ice crystals from forming and in other foods to help oil- and water-based ingredients mix. It can add slight sweetness, but it is usually used in very small amounts in keto recipes, so it does not contribute to the carb count.

Sweeteners

Allulose is a naturally occurring sugar derived from fruits like figs and jackfruit that contains 90 percent fewer calories than sugar and is about 70 percent as sweet as sugar. It is not digested by the body like normal sucrose, so it does not add carbohydrates. Allulose does not raise blood sugar or insulin and does not ferment in the gut. When baking with allulose, it is best to use one derived from monk fruit in breads and cakes. In frostings, a powdered cellulose sweetener is typically used. Both are found in different brand names, so read the labels carefully. Allulose tastes and performs just like sugar in baking. Sometimes it is the only choice for a certain recipe. In that case, I have specified allulose, and only allulose will give you the desired result. Otherwise, for granulated sweeteners you can safely use erythritol.

Erythritol is a sugar alcohol in granular form made from fermenting corn. It does not add calories and does not affect blood sugar. It can be purchased in granular or powdered form and is easy to use to replace sugar in baked goods. Be sure to purchase the one that is listed "non-GMO." Erythritol has a glycemic index of 0.

Liquid sweetener drops are made from stevia to give added sweetness.

Brown sugar substitute, or brown sweetener, provides a touch of extra flavor.

Fiber syrup gold is low calorie, gluten free and has only 2 net carbs. Half the calories of honey and syrup, with the same sweetness. It is made from erythritol and stevia.

Leili's Favorite Herbs and Spices

Saffron is a special herb made from the dried stigmas and styles of the saffron crocus, collected and processed by hand. Buy the "threads," not the powder, for the purest saffron. Typically, saffron is soaked in water before being added to other ingredients. It's expensive, but a little bit gives a classic flavor and color.

Rose water is a popular ingredient in Middle Eastern cooking. Look for culinary-grade rose water.

Tahini is sesame seed paste used in many Middle Eastern foods. It has a mild flavor and is widely available.

Za'atar is an herb mixture that includes dried sumac, salt and toasted sesame seeds. It has a mild but characteristic flavor of the Middle East.

Dried herbs are useful to have on hand in case you have no fresh herbs. Herbes de Provence is a nice mixture, as is za'atar, but you will also appreciate having dried dill and Italian herb mixtures on hand.

Must-Have Special Equipment

Stand mixer: Keto doughs are often stiff and require intensive kneading that will be easier with the stand mixer. Everything else mixes very smoothly and quickly in the stand mixer, especially cheesecake fillings.

Kitchen scale: So important for measuring. Accuracy is vital with baking, and only a correct weight of ingredients give the right proportions. Make friends with your scale!

Candy thermometer: For accurately measuring water temperature for yeast.

Bench scraper: This wide, firm tool made of metal or plastic is very useful when turning and rolling Leili's Perfect Pastry Dough (page 68). It's a good way to lift any sticky dough off the counter and also good for cutting and lifting portions of cooked or raw food.

Bread Baking Tips

I've tried to give detailed instructions on handling the keto doughs I have developed, but here are some general baking tips that will ensure your success, even if you are new to baking.

Always use a kitchen scale to weigh ingredients. You will find both volume and weight measurements in my recipes because many people are familiar with volume (cups, tablespoons, etc.), but **weighing your ingredients will give you much better control over your baking.** Flour volumes are affected by moisture, aeration and handling. It's best to use the scale and be exact. Any changes to the ratio of water to flour in any recipe, keto or not, will make changes in the final product. It's also much easier to double or halve ingredients on the scale.

You don't have to weigh each ingredient separately in a new bowl on your scale. You can use one bowl and just hit the "tare" button after weighing the bowl and again after each new ingredient addition.

Time and Temperature are part of the recipe and equally as important as the ingredients.

You will need a candy/yeast **thermometer** to measure the temperature of your liquids when using yeast. Don't rely on your fingertip, which could be off by quite a bit—and could kill or slow down the yeast.

The temperature of the water should be about 100°F (38°C). The temperature of your room and recipe ingredients should ideally be 68 to 72°F (20 to 22°C).

In a warmer environment dough will rise faster, but in a cooler environment it will develop more flavor while rising. My recipes give instructions on temperature for your success! Bread is very happy rising in a humid environment like a slightly warmed oven with the door ajar, a closed microwave or a proofing box.

Activate the yeast in warm water with a little sugar, honey or maple syrup according to the recipe. The small amount of sugar is needed to feed the yeast.

Patience is an ingredient for bread baking! Do not try to speed up the process or skip steps.

Bread dough should be kneaded until it is "lively" or pulls away from the sides of the bowl. Start the mixing with the paddle attachment on an electric mixer and then switch to the dough hook. At this time scrape down the sides of the bowl with a spatula and gather the dough into the center of the bowl. Watch the clock for kneading time as I have given exact instructions for each dough recipe.

If you have a bread machine, you can use the kneading cycle for this step.

After kneading, grease a large bowl and turn the dough into the bowl so that all dough surfaces are greased to keep them from drying out during rising. Then grease one side of a piece of plastic wrap, place it loosely over the bowl, then cover the bowl with a clean kitchen towel while the dough rises.

Dough typically rises until doubled in size during the first rising. Then it's time to shape the dough into loaves, buns, pizzas, etc.

Bread dough can rise in the refrigerator to develop more flavor! Cool rising can take between 4 and 24 hours. See the specific instructions in the Versatile Naan recipe (page 59).

Shaped dough should "proof" for the recommended time until it can hold the impression of a fingertip when touched. This varies by recipe, but I have included instructions with each one.

Follow the instructions for baking times and test the loaf for doneness by tapping on the top or bottom; it should sound hollow.

Egg washes are unique for certain recipes. An egg wash with water gives a shiny, dry look; butter makes the surface soft and shiny; egg with cream is used to make sweet doughs brown and shiny.

Acknowledgments

First and most importantly, I want to thank my dear husband Kaveh for believing that I have the skills and the talent to develop great recipes! He has always found ways to help me fit my work into our family life and has kept my goals within his sight.

I hold many others dearly in my heart for their help:

My dear sons, Hirad and Hirbod, really cooperated with me for my cookbook project!

My wonderful parents taught me the meaning of generosity and hospitality. In our home, good food was prepared with love.

My Instagram followers at @leili_keto have energized me for years with their enthusiasm and encouragement for my recipes and photos.

My publishers, Caitlin and Meghan—you helped my ideas come to life!

My friends Tina and Arash encouraged me through the details and read my manuscript.

Thank you!

Leili

About the Author

Leili Malakooti is an accomplished, award-winning graphic designer with a passion for good food. She thinks of cooking as both an artistic presentation and a delicious skill. She learned to cook with her mother in Iran, whose excellent food and beckoning table were legendary.

When a food lover lives and works in other countries, as Leili has done for the past fifteen years, it's impossible not to pick up new tastes, cooking methods and presentations. As an expat, she savored the dishes from her heritage; as an explorer, she blended the new tastes into her cooking. The fusion recipes that are Leili's favorites are those that feature flavors from the Pacific countries where she lived while working as a designer and model.

After health problems in two pregnancies, Leili turned to the keto diet because she feared the trend toward diabetes that ran in her family. She lost 100 pounds (45 kg) and has been in ketosis for five years. The artist in her was bored with the limited choices of the traditional keto diet, however, and soon she turned her skills toward developing more satisfying keto recipes.

The results are a blend of art and tradition, perfectly seasoned, perfectly tested, perfectly presented. This is keto food you want to eat and serve with pride!

Leili has been sharing her keto food creations via her Instagram account (@leili_keto) for more than three years and writes in both English and Farsi. After developing a recipe, she photographs her dishes in her home studio.

As a keto influencer, she has worked with a number of food companies in the United States to create recipes that they used to design new products. She is a recipe contributor for the well-known keto apps.

Leili is especially proud of her unique recipes for keto breads and doughs that are extraordinary.

Leili lives in Ohio with her husband Kaveh and her two active boys.

Index